Building Executive Function and Motivation in the Middle Grades

Building Executive Function and Motivation in the Middle Grades

A UNIVERSAL DESIGN FOR LEARNING APPROACH

Susanne Croasdaile

© 2023 CAST, Inc.

All rights reserved. No part of this publication may be reproduced, stored in a retrieval system, or transmitted in any form or by any means, electronic, mechanical, photocopying, recording, or otherwise, without the prior permission of the Publisher.

ISBN (paperback): 978-1-943085-00-2
ISBN (ebook): 978-1-943085-01-9

Library of Congress Control Number: 2023935905

Interior design, compostion, and editorial production by Westchester Publishing Services.

Cover by Endpaper Studio. Cover image: insta_photos/Adobe Stock.

Published by CAST Professional Publishing, an imprint of CAST, Inc., Lynnfield, Massachusetts, USA

For information about special discounts for bulk purchases, please email publishing@cast.org or visit publishing.cast.org

This book is dedicated to the instructional coaches and school leaders of all the model sites in Virginia's Superintendent's Regions 1 and 8. Your kindness, compassion, and determination to reflect and improve is inspiring.

Contents

Preface   xi

INTRODUCTION   1
     A little about UDL   2
     A little about research-based practices   4
     The importance of checklists for instructional models   4
     Barriers and obstacles to student success   8
     Use a checklist to address obstacles and develop expert learners   10

PART 1: Scaffolding Executive Function   13
     Scenario   13
     What is executive function?   19
     Step 1. Always scaffold working memory   25
         Importance of routine   26
         Think twice about whether your routines are working   27
     Step 2. Decide on critical routines to use across the year   28
         A routine is critical if it addresses prior problem areas or non-negotiables   28
         Always include a visual and possibly a mnemonic   30

Step 3. Plan and teach the First 20 Days routines   30
    Reflecting on the past helps decide future routines   31
    Work with others to increase the impact of the First 20 Days   34
    Introduce routines with low-risk content and situations, then increase the level of risk   35
    Communicate routines to administrators as well   36

Step 4. Progress monitor and scaffold/reteach the routines   37
    The struggle is real: Maintaining rigorous goals by using scaffolds   38

Planning steps to scaffold executive function   40

PART 2: Scaffolding Motivation   43

Scenario   44

Building internalized motivation in students   47
    Autonomy   48
    Mastery   50
    Purpose   51

Step 5. Offer multiple entry points to critical activities   54
    Many of us procrastinate   55
    How multiple entry points build internal motivation   56
    What does planning multiple entry points look like?   56
        Hook students   58
        Challenge students to engage in productive struggle   58
        Provide enough structure to minimize the risk of failure   59
        Spark further engagement   61

Step 6. Scaffold collaborative interactions   62
    Students who can collaborate effectively learned it from someone   63

How being in a collaborative community builds internalized motivation 64

What does fostering collaboration explicitly look like? 65

Step 7. Plan for mastery-oriented feedback 69

How mastery-oriented feedback builds internalized motivation 69

Teachers who give timely feedback often wear comfortable shoes 71

Breaking the plane and active supervision 71

What does mastery-oriented feedback look like? 72

Mastery-oriented feedback on preparation for the discussion 74

Mastery-oriented feedback on participation during the discussion 75

Mastery-oriented feedback to reflect on the discussion 78

PART 3: Pulling It All Together 83

Step 8: Set up and use an instructional calendar 83

Final Note	97
Acknowledgements	99
Appendix: The First 20 Days of School	101
About the Author	107
References	109
Index	113

Preface

IN 2005, I SUBMITTED my doctoral dissertation on teachers' reflective practice in social-organizational contexts to the University of Virginia and looked around for how to use my new skills as an educational researcher in a practical way to impact student outcomes. Action research, specifically practitioner research, was the answer, but . . . what, where, and how?

I was fortunate to work as a specialist in K–12 curriculum and instruction alongside a team of experienced systems change specialists during an important time in educational history. In the early 2000s, Virginia was in the midst of great change, having adopted and implemented K–12 state standards (similar to Common Core). Schools were interested in subgroup reporting and therefore inclusive practices. It was a prime time for working on instructional models.

Marzano's meta-analysis of research, *Classroom Instruction That Works*, was in everyone's hands, and educators were starting to recognize the letters PBS as representing Positive Behavior Support rather than just the home of *Sesame Street*. The time was right for big-picture planning, but we didn't have the right frameworks. Marzano's meta-analysis work with McREL wasn't structured to help educators make change in schools. PBS didn't include the academic side of the multi-tiered systems of support triangle yet. Those of us attempting to build coherence through instructional models were in need of vision.

Enter, stage right: Universal Design for Learning (UDL). I was working alongside Dr. Fran Smith, a member of the National UDL Task Force and part of the CAST UDL Professional Learning Cadre, and she opened the door to her UDL work, eventually inviting me to coteach and revise her UDL course at the George Washington University in Washington, DC. My world changed. A viable solution to our big-picture Tier 1 planning problem was to use UDL as a lens.

The structure of the guidelines was the key feature that helped with coherence-making: It didn't matter if a school had intended to use the UDL framework from the outset. School leaders could map Tier 1 initiatives to the guidelines and underlying UDL assumptions *at any time* and still achieve coherence. Who would recognize this? As a high school educator, I was surprised to find that the answer lay with the administrators and leadership teams of several middle schools.

Middle schools were (and are) caught in the middle of the accountability movement. Elementary schools invested in the early literacy needs of K–3+. High schools struggled with drop-out rates and retention. The middle grades continually experienced the highest accountability stress. The opportunities for investing in instructional models, therefore, were in intermediate schools, middle schools, and junior highs, since leaders of those institutions had to produce results through a coherent framework that increased year over year. This was the perfect environment for Tier 1 instructional model building with UDL as the lens.

Malcolm Gladwell writes in *Outliers*, "Extraordinary achievement is less about talent and more about special opportunity" (Gladwell, 2008, 76). As a partner in many schools serving Grades 5–9 in the early 2000s, I benefited from a special opportunity. I have stood beside stellar educators, rolled up my sleeves, and engaged in reflective practice cycles of action research with them. Four of these educators collaborated on this book.

First, Matoaca Middle School principal Gayle Hines and I spent hours planning this book as an addition to the research-to-practice literature on UDL. Gayle's experiences as a secondary teacher, department chair, central office curriculum specialist, beginning teacher mentor, and building administrator had given her a 360-degree view of how the UDL framework reduces barriers in the written and taught curriculum and scaffolds learner success.

Gayle returned from Harvard University's New and Aspiring Leaders Institute in 2014 full of questions and ideas about how her school would use the UDL Guidelines to look with fresh eyes at the goals, methods, materials, and assessments of the school's core curricula. I had only known her a short time when Gayle sent a 4:30 am text: "Who do I reach out to for UDL?" As a fellow early riser, I remember standing in my kitchen that morning and hearing the text message come in. I responded, "Me." That text exchange was the beginning of a journey that led to Gayle and me planning this book. Along the way, we've had many folks share their expertise.

Tricia Cook began her career as a special educator and has since served as the general education teacher in collaborative settings and has taught honors classes. She has served as English/Language Arts department chair, been a member of the leadership and school improvement teams, and coordinated the development of a schoolwide multi-tiered system of supports that includes an academic intervention, remediation, and enrichment block.

Samantha Layne has been a middle and high school science teacher with extensive experience teaching English language learners and students with disabilities. She has served as a department chair and on the school leadership team. Samantha is a national professional developer for the University of Kansas Center for Research on Learning's Strategic Instruction Model and currently leads a school-based peer coaching team. She also provides professional learning to teachers related to developing a school-based curriculum.

Stephanie Burton draws on over a decade of experience as a math teacher, school-based instructional coach, division-level math coach, and instructional designer. She has led innumerable professional learning sessions, written division curriculum, and supported school improvement teams at all levels and in many roles. Stephanie's wealth of experience and coaching expertise has helped her colleagues apply the UDL framework to their existing instructional model.

The work in this book comes from middle grade leaders who get up each day and try again, using increasingly deeper insight and hard-won experience. We all hope it helps the teachers and leaders who reach out to ask us how to get started building a UDL instructional model in their schools. I am honored to be the one who shares the action research experiences of our team of reflective practitioners with you.

Susanne Croasdaile

Building Executive Function and Motivation in the Middle Grades

Introduction

MIDDLE SCHOOLERS OFTEN struggle to transition from structured elementary schools to more independent secondary schools. In the primary grades, students soak up experiences energetically: First graders who encounter new information ask *more* questions than some of their teachers (and parents) want. Between ages 9 and 15, however, students' motivation declines, and they don't put forth the same effort to connect what they are seeing and doing to successful school and adult life (Gillet et al., 2012; Gnambs and Hanfstingl, 2016; Lepper et al., 2005). Those of us who have worked with fourth and fifth graders know that those students need help to become independent learners: We have to talk about what an independent learner is, set goals related to becoming independent learners, and structure experiences to help students see how they are growing.

In our experience, sometimes educators in sixth grade and beyond simply don't realize that students need *more* structure over time to develop their skills as independent learners, not less. As more intermediate and elementary schools become departmentalized at fourth and fifth grade, teachers in those grades may also unintentionally remove the scaffolds students need to become independent learners. We understand how this can happen and are sharing our experiences about how to ensure students get what they need to become successful independent learners.

Based on real-life examples of how educators have used the Universal Design for Learning (UDL) Guidelines and transformed learning for their students, *Building Executive Function and Motivation in the Middle Grades* provides a roadmap for anyone who seeks practical research-based strategies to help their students survive and thrive to become *expert learners* in the middle grades.

> **Expert learners are purposeful, motivated, resourceful, knowledgeable, strategic, and goal-directed . . . and it takes many years to build those skills!**

Highlighting practices related to students' executive function and sustained effort, this book is a useful addition to the toolkit of every classroom teacher, coach, and administrator.

A little about UDL

There are a few things that will be helpful if you are new to Universal Design for Learning. We call it *UDL* and we refer to it as a framework, which means it's a lens through which you view the world. Imagine wearing amber-tinted glasses: Your whole world would appear through those amber lenses. That's what we mean by applying the UDL framework: We look at the goals of curricula, the methods for achieving those goals, the materials students use to achieve the goals, and the formal and informal assessments of progress through a UDL lens.

Imagine a fifth-grade teacher is chatting with you about how she plans to have her students work on group presentations about frogs in the rainforest canopy. From experience, she knows she can't have them complete an old-school group research project in which each student takes notes from the class reading on index cards, and then they combine their knowledge on a group poster. If she tried that, she would be running around the room settling arguments and answering the question "What are we supposed to be doing?" while some of the students wandered around the room or took a nap. (By the way, many ninth-grade teachers would have something similar to say. Middle grade students take a long time to master these skills!)

To plan for the group presentations, this teacher uses a UDL lens and consults the UDL Guidelines on how to build expert learners (CAST, 2011). She uses the UDL Guidelines to plan the goals, methods, material, and assessments for the research project. She plans how to highlight the critical features students had been studying about frogs in the rainforest canopy and how to activate their background knowledge. She plans gradual release of responsibility for the skill of identifying supporting details and also the skill of writing a clear sentence for the research poster. She creates a checklist of tasks for each work period that are aligned to the project goals. The checklist supports students' emerging time-management skills and reminds them about the most important parts of the task. She trains them on how to carry out assigned group roles. Before they present their posters, she offers several short models of what the presentations can look like to reduce fear of the unknown and help them self-assess how their group is doing.

Although the curricular goal *appears* to be that students can present what they have learned about frogs in the rainforest canopy, we know that the most important learning has been about staying on task, communicating with others, following directions, and developing the growth mindset that independent learners need to persist during complex tasks. These social and emotional skills are the ones that seem the hardest to plan, but they pay off the most, for both our learners and ourselves as educators. Using a UDL lens helps us plan our curriculum to reduce barriers, include scaffolds, and still make it home in time to fix dinner (or at least pick up pizza).

If you have some experience with UDL already, you'll see that we primarily focus on UDL Guidelines 6 and 8 in this book (see page 92). Guideline 6 focuses on goal setting, strategy development, organization and memory, and monitoring one's own progress. Middle grade learners are in the thick of this learning. As we'll discuss later, some of them are in the process of learning from ages 9 to 15 but may not master what is addressed by Guidelines 6 and 8 until they reach age 25 or later.

UDL Guideline 8 focuses on helping students see that curricular goals matter and sometimes we have to do nonpreferred tasks. Life can't be all video games and naps, or there would be no food, clothing, or shelter for ourselves and our families. In addition, people feel a sense of fulfillment when they accomplish meaningful goals, so students in this age range need to learn that aspect of internal motivation. Guideline 8 also reminds us to provide supports so students can rise to high expectations, be contributing members of a learning community, and cultivate the growth mindset of a lifelong learner.

The overall goal of the UDL Guidelines is to remove barriers from the taught curriculum and build expert learners who are independent and successful. One key point in this book is that we need to normalize the *try, fail, try again* cycle of learning while also normalizing that effort is a necessary part of learning. Many aspects of modern life make success look effortless (thanks, social media), and as educators we need to teach students that *all* worthwhile tasks require effort.

A little about research-based practices

Before we begin, let us clarify: None of this is new! Over two decades ago, Marzano et al.'s first edition of *Classroom Instruction That Works* (2001), the go-to repository of evidence-based practices, highlighted the foundations of many of the steps for helping create expert learners you will see in this book. We were gratified to see that the third edition, *The New Classroom Instruction That Works* (Goodwin et al., 2023), includes the steps in this book that were absent from the first two editions of that influential research review.

In particular, it is good to see that *The New Classroom Instruction That Works* includes the importance of student-owned learning strategies and of scaffolding working memory and providing formative feedback. Other new focus areas include planning high-level questions in advance and using student responses as data for next steps, as well as spaced, mixed independent practice of higher-order thinking skills.

The importance of checklists for instructional models

Many evidence-based practices, therefore, are currently well known to us as teachers, coaches, and administrators. That's worth celebrating! But why are we not using those practices regularly and effectively? In his

Figure 1 Instructional Practices Checklist

To build strategic learners, scaffold executive function	Step 1	Always scaffold working memory
	Step 2	Decide on critical routines to use across the year
	Step 3	Plan and teach the "First 20 Days" routines
	Step 4	Progress monitor and scaffold/reteach the routines
To build purposeful and persistent learners, scaffold intrinsic motivation	Step 5	Offer multiple entry points to critical activities
	Step 6	Scaffold collaborative interactions
	Step 7	Plan for mastery-oriented feedback
To get started, pull it all together	Step 8	Set up and use an instructional calendar

2009 book *The Checklist Manifesto: How to Get Things Right*, surgeon Atul Gawande notes that professionals often know what the right moves are but fail to implement them in the moment. He argues that creating and using a checklist of the important steps, even if they seem obvious, helps professionals to hold themselves accountable for implementing those key practices with integrity at the right moment. This argument resonates with us as educators; We balance so many things simultaneously that it can be difficult to do all things well. This book uses the checklist approach to address a crucial issue: keeping our middle grade learners engaged throughout the tough years between ages 9 and 15.

This book will expand on the critical research-based practices in Figure 1. Readers with experience in implementing UDL will notice that we are focusing on UDL Guideline 6: Executive Functions and UDL Guideline 8: Sustaining Effort and Persistence. The real-life educators featured in this book all have experience in schools or on teams that use an *instructional model* based on the principles of UDL. These instructional models are checklists for best practices to implement with integrity.

How did we land on this checklist? It has been a decade-long journey of reflective practice. After the shift to standards-aligned instruction, we had focused on planning, implementing, and reflecting on multi-tiered systems of supports (MTSS), including positive behavior interventions and supports (PBIS, formerly known as PBS), for students in the middle grades. We continued to message that PBIS and MTSS address academic as well as behavior skills (Missouri Schoolwide PBIS, 2019). Using Universal Design for Learning as a framework, we continuously reflected on our practices to make sure the path to becoming expert learners moved from the shadows of a *hidden* curriculum available only to the privileged to an *explicit* curriculum made available to all.

We knew that for students to be successful academically, we needed to have the right interpersonal, prosocial, and compliance behaviors in place. So we were off to the races every year: making sure students had clear expectations across the school and in the classroom, practicing those behaviors at the beginning of the year (as well as after winter and spring breaks), providing some kind of verbal (and sometimes tangible) reinforcement for demonstrating them, and talking with staff about all of it to make sure we adjusted as needed. Theoretically, the instructional model was perfect.

We kept noticing, though, that we felt we were in the 1993 film *Groundhog Day* (directed by Harold Ramis), in which Bill Murray lives the same day over and over. Each day we would run into staff members with the same concerns. As our *Groundhog Day* continued for several years, we were inspired (or perhaps driven) to dig more deeply into why we continued to be so frustrated with our preadolescent and adolescent students. Then, one day, reading Fisher and Frey's (2011) work on the First 20 Days of school led to an aha moment:

> "They're in ____ grade; they should know how to do this by now," is a common complaint. It's true, and the chances are very good that they know how to engage in partner talk or how to work in a small group. It's likely that they've done these things dozens of times in previous years. But the truth is they do not know how to do it for you. (3)

While reading, we instantly thought of a colleague's story about going to traffic court after receiving a speeding ticket. With no court experience outside of watching TV, she arrived late and opened the door to a quiet courtroom. Seeing that the time on her watch was the arrival time printed on her summons, and that everyone was milling around as if waiting for someone, she quickly walked to the front of the courtroom and opened the low gate to approach the judge. Needless to say, there was a lot of excitement. After much ado, she explained that she thought they were waiting on her and was trying to speedily apologize for her tardiness. Wrong behavior, wrong time, lack of contextual expertise: She didn't know *how to do it for them*.

Reflecting on her story, we doubled down on making sure that every middle grade staff member was on the same page about *how* middle grade students (and adults who have to go to court, apparently) all need more explicit instruction on *what* to do, *when* to do it, *where* to do it, and *why* to do it (Archer and Hughes, 2011). Connecting the *how* to the *why* became a larger part of the process so that students could make better connections, and we felt like we were on the right path.

But lo and behold, even with those changes, *Groundhog Day* continued. Too many students in Grades 5–9 weren't getting started on tasks, following basic directions, persisting through minor obstacles, or working appropriately with peers. Although some situations improved with professional learning or administrative intervention, many staff members continued to have the same difficult days, many students continued to have the same challenging behaviors, and it was tough to predict which students were going to be successful and independent in demonstrating academic and interpersonal skills on any given day. Then, on March 13, 2020, a global coronavirus pandemic arrived, and we sent students to learn at home.

The world of teaching and learning shifted dramatically. Suddenly, just getting student attention was paramount. Can we get students to log in? Will students answer if I ask them a question? Are students even there, behind that blank screen? How do we get students to interact appropriately with us . . . or anyone else?

In the brick-and-mortar world, the refrain had been "They should know how to do this by now," but in the virtual world educators were open to discussion that students didn't *necessarily* know how to do *anything*. The pandemic changed our perspective on that, among many other things. To paraphrase Proust, we often say travel makes one see one's world in a different light. Interestingly, the daily troubleshooting and problem-solving around student academic and interpersonal behaviors in virtual instruction, during the pandemic, was akin to travel for many of us as locked-down educators grappled in unfamiliar territory.

> "The real voyage of discovery . . . consists not in seeking new landscapes but in having new eyes."
> Marcel Proust

And so at the beginning of the pandemic, we returned to the basics: students needed us to implement gradual release of responsibility so they could learn to demonstrate desired school behaviors (Fisher and Frey, 2011, 2021). We focused on a handful of engagement strategies (e.g., thumbs up) and taught them explicitly.

Fast-forward to August 2020: middle grade students had participated (or not) in a brief pilot of virtual instruction from March until the end of the school year. Socially distanced educators were sharing their thoughts online with one another at a rapid-fire pace. It felt like action research in the broadest sense of the term, and for the first time in a long time, teachers and administrators were open to trying drastically different instructional approaches just to survive. Routines that worked in person did not necessarily translate online. Students who were reliably compliant in person were suddenly absent . . . or demonstrating spectator behavior with little or no meaningful engagement.

Barriers and obstacles to student success

At the same time, disrupted routines and increased smartphone ownership seemed to be reducing *even more* the amount of sleep adolescents were getting and leading to dysfunctional and unsuccessful behaviors. A review of 76 research studies had already demonstrated that lack of sleep had a negative effect on social and psychological health, including loneliness; rumination, worry, and anxiety; and depression (Medic et al., 2017). Multiple findings in the same review also indicated that adolescents with excellent academic performance had earlier school night bedtimes than those with poor grades. We had suspected this for a while, but now we had evidence.

Pandemic isolation, smartphone use, and sleep deprivation from disrupted routines were causing our preadolescent and adolescent students to struggle with basic tasks and interactions, but those were outside our locus of control. What could we do *inside* our locus of control?

We returned to the UDL framework as we discussed schools' instructional models for the 2020–2021 school year. Gradual release of responsibility? Check. Highlighting critical features? Check. What was missing? Why were middle grade students struggling so much to display basic interpersonal behaviors, demonstrate even minimal effort, and activate even low levels of executive function? We turned to the social-emotional literature on adolescent learners to dig deeper.

In the past, we had used the social-emotional literature on preadolescents and adolescents to develop interventions, so this was familiar territory. The recent travel to the trials of virtual instruction, however, had opened our eyes to a new realization: Even with a typical range of learner variability, most of the UDL Guidelines 6 and 8 were either within middle grade students' zone of proximal development or *beyond* it (see CAST, 2011).

We reached a conclusion: The frustrations we had been hearing from staff for years were due to inappropriate expectations that students would be able to *independently* demonstrate executive function, set and attain goals, and regularly interact appropriately with others for a designated purpose. So much of the day for preadolescents and adolescents focuses on long-term goals and overcoming immediate desires. It's a training ground for the realities of adulthood.

Let's stop and think. An entire marketing field capitalizes on this lack of self-control (Moser et al., 2019). And, specifically, most rental car companies do not rent to customers under age 25 (Hawley, 2021). We were expecting students half that age to reliably manage themselves when the commercial world knows differently. Experts in the field of executive function had been telling us this for a while (Dawson and Guare, 2012, 2018). The issue wasn't low expectations; it was a fundamental misunderstanding of the need for long-term scaffolds *well beyond a typical sequence of gradual release of responsibility*—definitely from ages 9 to 15, but possibly past age 25.

In the following pages, we will illustrate some instructional moves that scaffold students to focus themselves, sustain effort, and persist through tasks, even when they are frustrated or bored. To do this, we will use UDL as a framework through which to plan and implement teaching and learning.

Even before the context of the pandemic closures, smartphones, and sleep deprivation, we knew that students in Grades 5–9 have been at risk of becoming distracted, unmoored, and unmotivated. In this age range, students may ignore or miss directions, resist working with others, and overlook or dismiss feedback. They often reject our exhortations to set goals and learn from productive struggle. All of this is predictable, so we do not need to wait for students to fail but instead can go ahead and plan instructional moves to scaffold desirable academic and social behaviors and distinguish the undesirable ones.

The importance of building student-owned expertise by replacing the hidden curriculum of school with an explicit one cannot be overcommunicated. Lisa Delpit proposed explicitly teaching skills as an important key to unlocking students' access to the culture of power. "If you are not already a participant in the culture of power, being told explicitly the rules of that culture makes acquiring power easier" (Delpit, 1988, 282). We agree. Middle grade students need to be empowered with tools to meet scaffolded high expectations, not just lectured or disciplined into compliance.

Use a checklist to address obstacles and develop expert learners

In this book, we will take a journey with a group of expert educators, and you'll walk away with a *Checklist Manifesto*–style sequence of steps to use tomorrow, next week, or in the coming year to develop expert learners. We've shared stories and offered instructional moves useful to teachers, coaches, leads, and administrators. Learning maps summarize what's in each section.

In Part 1, we will show how working memory is the secret ingredient underlying learning and that it is supported by chunking tasks into fluent routines with visuals and mnemonics. We will explore the First 20 Days approach to reducing the cognitive load on working memory while reaching rigorous academic and interpersonal goals. In Part 2, we will explore motivators and consider how to scaffold motivation during higher-order thinking tasks. We will explore multiple entry points for student learning, supports to help students talk to and work with peers, and structures for discourse that allow students to gain low-risk feedback that moves them closer to mastery. Finally, in Part 3, we will show how an instructional calendar pulls it all together when planning interpersonal and academic skills scaffolds for students.

Figure 2 Part 1 Learning Map

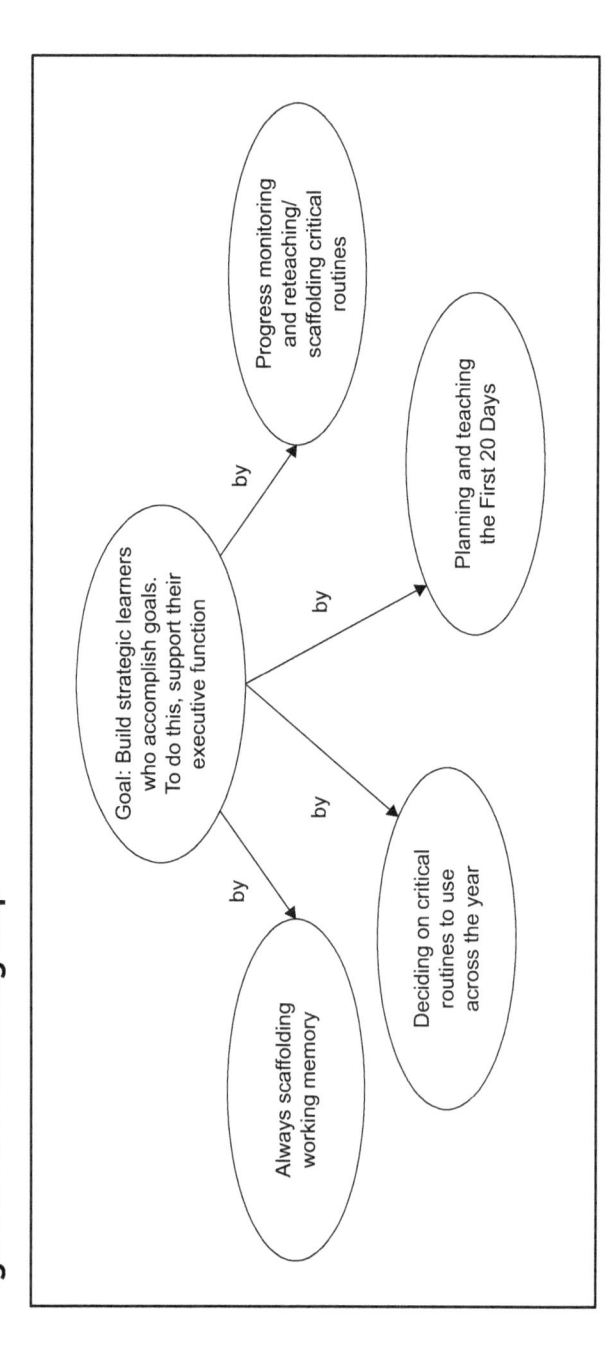

PART 1

Scaffolding Executive Function

SO MUCH OF what middle grade students need to do each day depends on their *executive function*, or the ability to self-monitor and carry out the steps of a plan effectively. Let's take a moment to follow a student around and see how many steps students have to keep in mind—and in how many contexts—to successfully navigate school.

Scenario

It's the first week of school at Midtown Junior High. With schedules in hand, students are following the cattle call of the bell system and moving through the halls. Teachers are standing at doorways, encouraging and ushering students along; administrators are collecting students from alcoves and restrooms, delivering them quickly and safely to their first block classes.

Students make their way into classrooms as the final bell rings and instruction begins. The school has a few non-negotiables for beginning-of-class routines—the agenda should be on the board, the learning target is posted and reviewed with students—but students with eight classes likely have eight different sets of academic and behavioral expectations conveyed either explicitly or implicitly by their teachers. What does this

Figure 3 Michael's Schedule

A Day	B Day
Family and Consumer Sciences Almond	*Pre-Algebra* Olivier/Gordon
Civics Miller	*English/Language Arts 8* Anderson
Art I Jones	*Spanish I* Williams
Physical Science Garcia	*Health and Physical Education* Davis

look like for a student? Let's follow Michael, an eighth grader at Midtown Junior High, to find out.

Midtown Junior High has an A/B alternating block schedule (see Figure 3). At the first bell of his A day, Michael enters Mrs. Almond's family and consumer sciences classroom. As he sits in his assigned seat, he looks at the agenda on the whiteboard for the Do Now. He looks around the room and sees pocket folders in other students' hands and on their desks. He remembers he should have picked up his pocket folder from the rolling cart on his way in, so he gets up to navigate the incoming tide of tardy students to retrieve his folder. Michael settles back in his seat to complete the Do Now that is already in his folder while Mrs. Almond finishes taking attendance at her desk at the back of the room. She remains seated as she reads aloud the agenda on the board at the front of the room, then circulates among students to check that they started the first task.

Let's fast-forward to tomorrow, so we can see Michael's first block class on B day. At the first bell, Michael enters Mr. Olivier and Ms. Gordon's cotaught pre-algebra classroom. He puts his bag on the desk he sat at last time, walks across the room to get his binder from the shelf on the back wall, makes his way back to his seat, opens to a new page behind the second tab of his binder, and starts copying down the Bellringer from the Promethean board. Mr. Olivier circulates in the room to monitor progress and offer help while Ms. Gordon takes attendance at her desk. Michael asks Mr. Olivier a few questions as he passes. After a few minutes,

Ms. Gordon reviews the agenda on the whiteboard, and then Mr. Olivier starts reviewing the Bellringer on the Promethean board.

Michael has two different beginnings to his class routines in two different classrooms on his A and B days. Both classrooms are typical, and neither is better than the other. One key to Michael being successful this year will be his mastering the routines of every class. How is he doing? Let's stay with Michael as he leaves pre-algebra and heads to his next class. He walks into Ms. Anderson's English/language arts class, and she greets him at the door with a smile. He jokes with her about not being fully awake yet and then heads into the room.

He walks to the seat Ms. Anderson assigned him and retrieves his composition book and binder from his backpack. He checks the Warm Up section of the board and copies the writing prompt into his composition book. The room is quiet. After Michael is done writing, he looks at the agenda on the board. Ms. Anderson has written several things on the agenda today:

- binder check during a reading activity
- independent writing activity that students begin after completing the reading activity
- work as partners on a project started in the last class session

After taking attendance, Ms. Anderson reviews the agenda, pointing to each item on the board as she speaks, and calls on students to repeat back to her the directions. She then points again to the first item. She announces that she will walk around and check binders while students read independently. The reading activity involves skimming a nonfiction text, annotating it while reading, and then answering questions using text evidence from the annotation. Although this is not a new skill for these eighth graders, Ms. Anderson verbally reviews how to skim a text: look at the title and headings, read the introduction, read the first sentence of every paragraph, look at the other text features, read the conclusion, and make sure you know what it's about. She then holds up the questions that go with the passage and reminds students to use evidence from their annotation to support their answers. After Ms. Anderson asks whether there are questions about what to do now, she moves to the front row and leans over a student's binder to start the binder check.

Michael gets his binder out and asks his neighbor about what they are supposed to be doing right now. The neighbor responds that he is making up the worksheet he missed last class, then looks back down at his paper and keeps working. Michael looks around the room and sees students looking down at their binders. He flips through his binder, doesn't see anything missing from last class, and leans back in his chair to wait for Ms. Anderson to get to him for the binder check. He's feeling pretty good about the class so far and he likes how Ms. Anderson keeps the room calm and organized. He looks up at the ceiling and smiles faintly, feeling relaxed and comfortable.

However, when Ms. Anderson scans the room and sees Michael, she sees a student who is not following directions. Clearly, the other students are looking down in their binders doing the task she just went over: skimming the nonfiction text that was handed out and placed in the binder during the last class session. Ms. Anderson wonders, "Why is Michael lounging and looking at the ceiling? Is this laziness? Refusal to comply with directions? I thought he liked this class. What do I do with him?"

As educators, we know that this is a tough moment for Michael and Ms. Anderson. If this were a "Choose Your Own Adventure" book, we might "turn to page 8 if she walks over to quietly ask him what he should be doing," or "turn to page 26 if she calls loudly across the room to tell him to get back to work." But this is a very real scenario for many of us, so let's stop and think about what might really be going on here.

It's easy to start pointing fingers. We know Ms. Anderson had an organized lesson plan with an agenda. She gave students clear directions and checked for understanding. We also know that Michael is still hanging in there during the second block of the day after a busy first block, arrived on time and prepared for class with his composition book and binder, and immediately complied with what he *thought* was the task. He used two strategies to ensure he was behaving correctly: asking a neighbor and scanning the room. He is comfortable and in a class he enjoys.

What could support Michael in this situation? After all, by midmorning, Michael has successfully navigated two different start of class routines and has an organized binder in front of him. He looked at the agenda when he came in but is now off-task. What can be done to further scaffold Michael? The challenge here is that Michael is not being successful with the complexities of the agenda item. He did the first part, but not the rest. Ms. Anderson did a lot of talking, and he is not using the written agenda effectively.

Let's rewind for a moment and restart the scenario. This time, Ms. Anderson breaks the concurrent tasks of the binder check and the reading activity into two parts:

1. Put your binder on your desk.

2. Give me a thumbs up when you are ready for the reading activity directions.

After scanning the room and getting thumbs up from all students, she points to three steps she has added to the agenda on the board:

1. Skim page 4 in your binder using your THIEVES chart.

2. Read and annotate page 4 using your text annotation chart.

3. Answer the questions on the back of page 4 using text evidence from your text annotation.

She reads each step while having students locate the relevant pages in their binders. She reviews the steps of THIEVES (see Figure 4) while students look at their chart. She repeats this for the text annotation chart. Ms. Anderson then has students explain the task to a neighbor. She circulates to make sure all have started before she begins her binder check.

It is basically the same lesson, so what really changed?

- First, Ms. Anderson scaffolded student attention. The binder task is simply logistics, so she handled that and moved on. The reading activity applies to previous learning, so she reviewed that learning and checked readiness before students began the independent task.

- Next, she used *chunking*. Chunking means teaching students *routines* that are standardized within the context. Although each routine may consist of many steps, the routine is handled as one task that is scaffolded in the agenda on the board and through charts in the binder. Like cooks who glance briefly at a recipe to be reminded of next steps, students refer to the agenda and charts to remind them of the routine.

Figure 4 THIEVES Routine Mnemonic

THIEVES
skim nonfiction *for 3 minutes* **before** *reading*

Title	• What is the title? • What do I already know about this topic? • Does the title express a point of view? • What do I think I will be reading about?
Headings	• What does this heading tell me I will be reading about? • What is the topic of the paragraph beneath it? • How can I turn this heading into a question that is likely to be answered in the text?
Introduction	• Is there an opening paragraph (perhaps *italicized*)? • Does the first paragraph introduce the text? • What does the introduction tell me I will be reading about? Do I know anything about this topic already?
Every 1st sentence	• What do I think this text is going to be about based on the 1st sentence in each paragraph?
Visuals and vocabulary	• Does the text include photographs, drawings, maps, charts, or graphs? • What can I learn from the visuals in the text? • How do captions help me better understand the meaning? • Is there a list of key vocabulary terms and definitions? • Are important words *italics* or **boldface** type throughout the text? Do I know what they mean?
Ending	• What does the ending or conclusion tell me I will be reading about?
So what?	• Why is this important?

If Michael has learned to use THIEVES, the text annotation chart, and a routine for answering questions with text evidence from his annotation, he is following three chunked steps in the agenda and is able to feel independent and successful. He is unlikely to get lost in the individual verbal directions from Ms. Anderson.

Now, let's step back and explore why this works, and how the answer is grounded in working memory, the key to executive function.

What is executive function?

As we've seen with Michael, students have to keep a lot of steps in mind, in a lot of different locations, to successfully make it through the day. Much of what middle grade students need to do each day depends on their executive function, or the ability to self-monitor and carry out the steps of a plan effectively. Before we think about what to do for Michael and the students in your school, let's think about how our own brains work.

One of the best applications of executive function for most of us occurs in our kitchens. Cooking tasks have often been used to analyze the executive function of individuals (Doherty et al., 2015). Since executive function refers to how we set appropriate goals, plan how to reach those goals, organize materials and tasks to reach the goal, manage time well, and adapt and adjust when needed without losing motivation, we can all put ourselves in a situation where we started cooking and found that we had to adjust our plans to get to our goal of delicious and attractive food! See Figure 5 for examples of this.

Picture yourself in the kitchen making a complex meal: Maybe it's Thanksgiving, or Sunday dinner, or that pad Thai recipe you've always wanted to make. Perhaps some of the food goes on the grill on the patio while some is boiling on the stove. Is something defrosting in the refrigerator or microwave? Do you need to stir the item on the stove every so often while checking the oven? And what happens if your phone rings? Let's stop and think.

- Do you know what you need to do?
- Do you have the utensils and ingredients you need?
- Are you managing time and multiple tasks well?
- Can you get back on track when you get distracted?

Figure 5 Executive Function and Cooking Analogy

Executive Function	Cooking
Set appropriate goals	<ul><li>What do you want to cook?</li><li>When do you want it?</li><li>How much do you want to make?</li></ul>
Plan how to reach those goals	<ul><li>What specific recipes have you selected?</li><li>How will you access them during cooking?</li><li>Do you need to learn a technique?</li><li>How will you get the tools and ingredients?</li><li>Are tools and ingredients easily accessible while you cook?</li><li>When will you start so that you finish on time?</li><li>What needs to be done first? Last?</li></ul>
Managing steps in reaching the goals	<ul><li>Do you need to practice ahead of time and make the recipe more than once?</li><li>Can you prepare anything ahead of time?</li><li>What will you do if something goes wrong?</li></ul>
Progress monitor and adjust	<ul><li>How will you know you're on the right track?</li><li>What will you do if you're not?</li><li>How will you adjust your actions?</li><li>How will you adjust the recipe?</li></ul>

All these steps test your executive function capacity. Much of this work also depends on your *working memory*, or the ability to temporarily hold multiple pieces of information in mind while doing a task. You might recognize the concept of working memory from the phone number rule: It was believed that we can keep about seven things in our working memory at any given time, which is the number of digits in a local phone number. The real number is currently understood to be probably closer to four (Doolittle, 2013). The truth is, if we do not do something with information, like write it down or anchor it to existing knowledge ("I knew a pumpkin was a fruit, but now I know why"), our working memory wipes itself clean when the next piece of information comes along. To illustrate the challenges of working memory in real life, picture this:

> *Your phone rings as you're getting in the car after work. A family member needs four items from the grocery store for tonight. You suddenly remember you need two things as well. They also gave you the name of a prescription to pick up at the store's pharmacy counter. As you pull out of the parking lot, the low-gas light comes on. You decide that you can use the gas pumps at the grocery store and handle all your errands at once.*

> *An hour later, you arrive home with four of the items the family member called about and both of the ones you needed, but not the prescription or the gas. Irritated, you think back to being distracted by a text message and not making it to the pharmacy counter at the back of the busy store. When you returned to the car in the congested parking lot, there was an opening in traffic to take your typical right turn onto the main road, so you exited the parking lot without remembering to drive to the other side of the store, where the gas pumps were located.*

Sound familiar? Let's spend a moment on working memory. We scaffold our own working memory all the time. When we feel that the cognitive load of a task is getting to be too much, we make lists, write on our hands with a marker, come up with mnemonic strategies . . . and still forget or miss things frequently. (By *cognitive load* we mean the amount we can hold in our brain before it can't take anymore. There is a well-known *Far Side* cartoon in which a student raises his hand and says, "May I be excused? My brain is full." That's a joke about cognitive load.)

Researchers have used the analogy of different sizes of sticky notes to represent different learners' working memories (Alloway & Alloway, 2015). Some people's sticky notes are large and can hold lots of steps or information, while others' are small and can hold much less. After childhood, a person's sticky note does not grow much, and those who do not develop coping strategies may experience a negative impact. In fact, working memory has been correlated to IQ (Gathercole et al., 2008).

Developing strategies for executive function that support working memory is critical to becoming an expert learner. Knowing how the brain works helps us to see how to scaffold it until it is able to fluently handle tasks. One important fact that we all benefit from keeping in mind is this: Our brain changes. This is what is meant by brain plasticity. Although our neurons don't change, the connections between them do: The ones we frequently use together build stronger connections, and the ones we don't use together become disconnected from one another (Meyer et al., 2014, 53). Fluency in behavior means physical connections in the brain: It's no joke that we need to "use it or lose it." Habits and routines impact brain connections enormously during childhood and adolescence: The behaviors students practice now become the habits of a lifetime.

As we noted in the Introduction, students between ages 9 and 15 are increasingly disengaged in academic tasks, which means they are *doing something else*. Many learners may be losing out on developing academic skills and identities by practicing disengaged behaviors over and over for hours and hours (Dawson & Guare, 2012). Their brains are making strong neural connections that reinforce *not* initiating tasks right away, *not* asking questions about the task, *not* attempting and revising in the face of setbacks, and *not* engaging in discourse and interacting with peers for academic purposes.

If we can help children become familiar with the terminology and definitions associated with executive skills, then they, too, can take ownership of the concepts, see their own behavior in terms of a set of skills that can be improved on, and even help devise their own strategies for doing this work. In their work on executive function, Dawson and Guare (2018) note:

> When we work with teachers now, they are more likely to understand that the students they are concerned about are not lazy but lack task initiation or sustained attention, and they're less likely to see them as willfully misbehaving and more likely to see them as having problems with response inhibition or emotional control. . . . We stressed that these skills take a long time (25 years or more!) to develop fully, and we've counseled patience to our audiences. We emphasized the need to create environments in which children with weak executive skills could be successful. (vii)

We have a range of learners in front of us at all times. Acknowledging differences in working memory is a great illustration of how educators who apply the UDL lens see learner variability as normal. Our middle grade learners might be disorganized and leave their papers everywhere. They may be forgetful when they go to the office to drop off their excuse for absence and come back with a hoodie they saw in the lost and found box but still have the excuse note in their hand. They may be unprepared when they arrive with a binder and loose-leaf paper but nothing to write with, even though when you saw them last they had a pencil case. Or they write the first sentence of an essay but nothing else during 20 minutes of writing time. In each of these situations, the students are showing how they need different types of support to scaffold their working memory and executive function skills (see the box "Working Definitions of Selected Executive Skills").

> **Working definitions of selected executive skills**
>
> **Dawson and Guare (2012, pp. 8–9) clarify how executive function (EF) refers to a constellation of skills that are both hereditary and developed through experience and practice. These critical skills include:**
>
> - **Response inhibition:** the capacity to think *before* you act; the ability to resist the urge to say or do something that allows you to have time to evaluate a situation and how your behavior might affect it;
>
> - **Working memory:** the capacity to hold information in memory *while* performing a complex task; includes the ability to draw on past learning or experience to apply to the situation at hand or to project into the future;
>
> - **Sustained attention:** the capacity to continue paying attention to a situation or task *in spite of* distractibility, fatigue, or boredom;
>
> - **Organization:** the capacity to create and maintain systems to handle information or materials;
>
> - **Task initiation:** the capacity to begin tasks quickly and efficiently;
>
> - **Metacognition:** the capacity to step back and observe yourself problem-solving in a situation, including asking yourself, "how am I doing" and "how did I do?" This includes observing others and trying out their skills in your actions.

Think of the organizational systems we use as professionals and as effective coordinators of our home lives. Organizers, reminder systems, calendars, lists—some of us have an office-supply addiction that has developed over time. People have an affinity for things that make them feel organized and successful because these systems or supports help to reduce stress and give hope that things will be manageable. When we provide our young learners with the supports that they need, they in turn will develop a similar sense of self-efficacy and feel that same hope.

At the same time, we want to help them build coping strategies related to working memory. We do Michael and other students no favors when we perform tasks for them and scaffold in a way that removes the productive struggle.

Let's look at another real-life example. Even as expert learners ourselves, we might write a list of tasks related to doing our taxes, go online to purchase tax software, but then become distracted by other shopping tasks or the need to find a new Pandora station of music to get in the right tax preparation mood. This is normal and everyone experiences it. Emotionally, we might get frustrated at the thought that tax preparation is pulling us away from more preferred tasks (like taking a walk on the one nice weekend day we have had) or an urgent task (like tending to a crying baby). We might then procrastinate and not finish our taxes because we didn't revise our strategy, perhaps by chunking the task and giving ourselves breaks.

The point of this example is to show that challenges with working memory and goal completion are normal—we are all challenged by working memory tasks! Although we have looked at the short-term goal scenarios of running errands and doing our taxes, working memory and mental organization apply to longer-term goals as well.

We have all experienced setting a big, hairy, audacious goal ("I'm going to grow all our own vegetables this year!"). If we're expert learners, we then move to strategic planning: Research online, get a gardening book, sign up for a class at the rec center, visit a friend with a green thumb, or call a relative who has had a successful garden in the past. We then plan and plot (and probably spend a lot of money on materials) to prepare to reach the goal. After all that, life happens, and we find ourselves buying tomatoes and green beans at the grocery store in July, feeling frustrated with ourselves. We can replace this scenario with one involving the unused kayak in the garage or the treadmill used as a clothes hanger in the bedroom.

As you read this, you may be saying to yourself, "Forget our students—*adults* have trouble with staying on task for goals like this!" We agree: This is a skill that develops after years of strategy development and practice. And, of course, there is tremendous learner variability in how people set short- and long-term goals, plan and manage their strategies, and reflect on progress to revise their course.

We need to constantly remind ourselves, by thinking of our own experiences, that our working memory sharply limits our executive function capacity. We are continually dealing with new tasks that may not yet be automatic or fluent for us; they slow us down or even derail us from our goals. An illustration of this is how most days you can drive to work and have a conversation with your passenger while the radio is on, but in bad weather you turn off the radio and ask the passenger (hopefully nicely) to stop talking because your entire concentration is required for the novel (not automatic) task of driving in traffic during bad weather.

Here's what all of us know: Our middle grade students simply lack automaticity in most complex situations. They don't know *how to do it for you*. Regardless of the size of their working memories, they just don't have a lot of experience with multistep tasks and therefore are often unable to determine where to begin or are easily derailed after starting. English language learners have the added burden of their working memories being consumed with processing the language. In addition, students with disabilities such as attention-deficit disorder may be far behind the starting line for executive function.

We can help our middle grade students by scaffolding multistep tasks so it is easier to get back on track when distracted or derailed. Let's look at the first of the steps for scaffolding learners.

Step 1. Always scaffold working memory

Learners with small working memory sticky notes (capacity) have a hard time following multistep directions, since only a few steps fit in the small space. They also have trouble with activities that require them to process information *at the same time as* they hold on to it. Education as a field has been slow to apply current research widely in schools, so many of us have not had any opportunity to reflect on and implement classroom methods to support working memory (Meyer et al., 2014, 104–105).

What does low working memory look like to a teacher? It can look like a student who is being quiet, even in groups. It can look like making minimal progress academically but not for any clear reason (Holmes, 2018). We might think it is an internalized behavior. It is actually related to missed instruction due to working memory.

In some cases, our students do not even struggle: They have already forgotten the second step after completing the first one. They may look around the room to see what others are doing, follow what they see, and jump back in on step four.

We also have to consider the perspective of our students who are English language learners. Put yourself in their shoes, and imagine answering a reading comprehension question in a new language: You hear a sentence out loud, then you have to remember the words, translate them in your head, remember the question, and then determine the answer based on your analysis of the translated words *and* comprehension of their combined meaning.

So what do we do to make sure we address something we can't even see? The first answer is to *chunk* steps, like Ms. Anderson did in Michael's class. Chunks are fewer pieces to write on the working memory sticky note: A routine transforms a seven-item task list into a single task. Many of us know this because we can make coffee or drive home and not remember the steps on the way. It's routine, and the brain treats a routine as a fluent task because the connections between the neurons are strong. So, to scaffold students' working memories (of various sizes), it is imperative that we chunk activities into routines.

Importance of routine

Let's step back and think about the importance of routine in schools. It's common educational parlance to say that *we, as teachers*, chunk tasks, but what does that really mean? We need to make sure we're setting up the student to handle the chunks of tasks, not simply acting as the teacher and providing continual adult support. Our goal is for students to achieve independence. We need the power of routines to help students be successful.

Again, let's connect this situation to our own lives. We can talk on the phone and make dinner as long as we have made that recipe before in that kitchen. That's because we're dealing with *routine* tasks. We've talked on that phone before, we've made that recipe before, we've located ingredients and tools in that space before. These are routines for us, since they are chunks of steps that have moved from our short-term memory (sticky note) to our long-term memory. We are expert learners with these complex tasks in this environment.

If we move to a new kitchen, however, we will not be in a routine anymore. Each step calls on our working memory, which may make us start talking to ourselves ("Now I need a slotted spoon. Slotted spoon. Where are you? There you are"), or adapt in other ways to maintain information in our working memory as we work through a routine task in a novel environment. We may either narrate these steps to the person on the phone or hang up because now is just not the right time for the phone call!

Think twice about whether your routines are working

As educators, we often think that we have certain routines in place. Often, we do not. Some students have larger sticky notes than others, and it's gratifying to see them be successful. Some students have learned similar routines in the past, and they are generalizing from them. But in general, we do not spend nearly enough time on moving critical academic, interpersonal, and organizational routines from students' working memory sticky notes to their long-term memory. That's why students aren't successful with our routines and procedures, and we feel like we're in *Groundhog Day*. As Fisher and Frey pointed out, the students know how to do these things; they just do not know how to do them *for you*.

So how do we implement routines and procedures so that students' brain networks are creating the strong, practiced pathways that expert learners have? We need to decide what stable routines students will use most often (these will change only minimally), create and share the routines in a way that students can easily refer to, and teach each routine so students can use it independently. These routines are ways to deliver information that minimize working memory loads (Elliott et al., 2010; Gathercole & Alloway, 2007; Gathercole et al., 2016).

Step 2. Decide on critical routines to use across the year

As we think about routines, think about the life of an educator. Successful educators have routines to start the day, check email and other electronic messages, organize daily agendas and weekly calendars, organize papers, and focus on independent tasks despite distractions. We often use verbal rehearsal of the routines to scaffold our working memory ("OK, I need to answer this parent, then go get this student for a check in, then get through this paperwork") then write down the tasks to check off before we forget. We may keep the note in our hands so we will not get distracted. We may organize our desks or daily checklists to reflect our preferred routines. Now think about our students. How do students become fluent in eight different opening-of-class routines?

Think about the most important repeated routines in which your students should become independent. Name each routine so you can cue students to use it. Common categories include:

- Start-of-class routines (e.g., warm-up)
- Learning routines (e.g., word problem solving)
- Communication and collaboration routines (e.g., think-pair)
- Organizational routines (e.g., binder)
- Classroom and school logistics routines (e.g., bathroom)

A routine is critical if it addresses prior problem areas or non-negotiables

How many do you need? Well, you need more than one but fewer than 20! Start from the length of a class period and then think about what typical days look like. What critical activities do the students need to do? Review the categories above and decide which has the highest impact. The box below provides some ideas to get you started. If you identify one start-of-class routine, one problem-solving or annotation strategy, one or two organization strategies, and two or three partner/small group interaction strategies, you have decided on about six class-wide strategies to explicitly teach to the class. As you get to know your students and as they understand your expectations, you and they can adjust the strategies to meet individual needs. But first, make sure you provide flexible models of skilled performance. These examples demonstrate for students what it looks like to do the routine correctly in a range of circumstances and allow you to highlight critical concepts.

Planning your critical routines for the year

Doug Lemov's *Teach Like a Champion* (2021) includes many routines, such as Turn and Talk and Silent Solo, that are worth adding to the First 20 Days. Himmele and Himmele's *Total Participation Techniques* (2017) is another go-to resource for many educators for routines. Ron Berger's EL Education team has an excellent set of routines to explore in *Management in the Active Classroom* (Berger et al., 2015).

Examples of start-of-class routines	Examples of learning strategies	Examples of organization strategies	Examples of peer interaction strategies
Warm up, Do now, Bellringer	Understand, Plan, Solve, Check problem-solving strategy	Binder with table of contents or tabs	Turn to your neighbor
Problem of the day or Sustained silent reading	Notice and Note text annotation strategy	Notebook with table of contents	Think-Pair
Entrance or entry tickets	POW-TREE prewriting strategy	Student task calendar with planning steps and deadlines	SCORE cooperative group strategy

Always include a visual and possibly a mnemonic

Once you know your routines, create a visual and (if possible) a mnemonic of the steps of each one. The University of Kansas Center for Research on Learning's Strategic Instruction Model (KU-CRL SIM) is a good resource for graphic devices and instructional sequences (Deshler & Lenz, 2004). In addition, two books of visual scaffolds are worth owning. For English/language arts, science, social studies, and career and technical education teachers, Linder (2014) has created *Chart Sense*, an excellent resource full of visuals and mnemonics for scaffolding literary and informational text analysis, including evidence and argument. A companion text has visuals for writing, including charts for arguments and opinions, informational texts, narratives, research, and editing (Linder, 2015).

You can be as flexible as you want with your routines, but you need a visual and a mnemonic so students know *how to do it for you* and can use those scaffolds to become fluent and successful in multistep tasks. That's how you will know you have helped them *chunk* the activity.

Step 3. Plan and teach the First 20 Days routines

One of our strongest recommendations is to carefully plan out all the routines that students will need and select the most critical ones to teach in the first month of school. We call this the *First 20 Days*, signifying the number of school days in the first four weeks of the academic year. If you have students every other day, we know it's really 10 days, but either way it's the amount of time you have to invest in building automaticity so the working memory sticky note is not overtaxed all the time.

Gayle Hines, an experienced middle school principal and former central office curriculum specialist, recommends that every teacher in the school plan and teach the First 20 Days (G. Hines, personal communication, July 12, 2022) to establish routines and procedures to create a "safe space" for students. "It is first about building relationships, but then also being consistent in your routines and procedures and following what it is that you set out," said Hines. Such routines don't have to be numerous or complicated. It's just about making the procedures and expectations clear to students—this works as much for students as it does for teachers. As Hines says, "Teachers struggled just as much during the COVID pandemic as the students, and some of them are struggling to understand why students are struggling."

For Hines, setting the tone in the First 20 Days can help build the trust in student–teacher relationships. She suggests that teachers might consider asking themselves such questions as

> What does it look like to be a scholar in this school?
> How do I interact with other students?
> How do I interact with adults?
> How do I have a conversation: first with one person, then with more people?

Hines points out that we should keep in mind that students may not have these skills when they first arrive at the schools, so it's important to set up low-risk situations for students. Hines concludes, "The First 20 Days just sets us up for success. Students are going to learn how to be scholars in our school."

Reflecting on the past helps decide future routines

The simplest way for an experienced educator to plan the First 20 Days is through reflection. What have students struggled with in the past? What actions or tasks did you hope students would be fluent in—but they were not? Those are the ones to start with. Let's take a look at an example.

Mr. Miller, a social studies department chair who teaches eighth-grade civics on an A/B schedule, is planning out the First 20 Days for his class. He wants to use it as an example for his department during teacher work week, so he's being explicit about his decision-making. He has narrowed his focus to several key routines for middle grade learners:

1. Talk to your neighbor (TTYN) protocol
2. Small group discussion protocol
3. Evidence protocol, such as *How do you know?*
4. Sentence stems, especially for his students who are English language learners

5. Strategic Instruction Model (SIM) higher-order thinking routines:
   - Concept Comparison Routine (Bulgren et al., 1995)
   - Teaching Decision-Making (Bulgren, 2018)
   - Cause and Effect (Bulgren, 2014)
   - Teaching Cross-Curricular Argumentation (Bulgren, 2021)

Mr. Miller can't get all of this in during the 10 instructional periods, so he's going to have to make some tough decisions. Based on his experiences in previous years, he brainstormed which standards his students need in the first four weeks. Students should communicate effectively in week 1, organize notebooks in week 2, use evidence in an argument in week 3, and defend their arguments with evidence in week 4 (see Figure 6). His school uses SIM and *Teach Like a Champion* routines in their professional learning, so he's naming some of the routines in ways the students and his department will recognize. After he has chosen the routines that best support the desired student outcomes, he has to plan how to teach them.

Now Mr. Miller is ready to deconstruct and make daily decisions about what will move the cognitive load from the sticky note of working memory to long-term memory, or fluency. This is how we ensure that the students *know how to do it for us*. The goal is to make sure students:

- won't have more than two steps to keep in mind
- can use visuals as scaffolds
- learn mnemonics to aid retrieval

Figure 6 Mr. Miller's Brainstormed Standards

Week 1	Use sentence stems for supporting evidence.	Set expectations for oral communication.
Week 2	Use an analysis tool to analyze and interpret artifacts and primary and secondary sources.	Organize notebooks.
Week 3	Construct informed, evidence-based arguments from multiple sources.	Determine multiple cause-and-effect relationships that impact political and economic events.
Week 4	Use a decision-making model to analyze and explain the costs and benefits of a specific choice.	Defend conclusions, orally and in writing, to a wide range of audiences, using evidence from sources.

Figure 7 Mr. Miller's Selected Standards

Week 1	✓ Use sentence stems for supporting evidence.	✓ Set expectations for oral communication.
Week 2	Use an analysis tool to analyze and interpret artifacts and primary and secondary sources.	✓ Organize notebooks.
Week 3	✓ Construct informed, evidence-based arguments from multiple sources.	✓ Determine multiple cause-and-effect relationships that impact political and economic events.
Week 4	Use a decision-making model to analyze and explain the costs and benefits of a specific choice.	✓ Defend conclusions orally and in writing to a wide range of audiences, using evidence from sources.

Since on-task student talk is critical for his standards, Mr. Miller decides to prioritize the talk to your neighbor and small group discussion protocols of the four key routines listed earlier. He adds them to the calendar first.

Mr. Miller calls a colleague in his social studies department to be a sounding board. The two of them look at the standards (Figure 7) and what the standards tell them about what routines to use in the classroom. Once his colleague is up-to-speed, Mr. Miller shares his thinking so far about the First 20 Days. They talk about how their students who are English language learners and students with disabilities struggle to make themselves understood in discussion but are concerned about pacing. The colleague suggests combining key routines 3 and 4 into a larger, connected routine. They call this routine *accountable talk* based on what they have learned in graduate classes and in their division's professional learning sessions (Michaels et al., 2016).

Although Mr. Miller has four SIM higher-order thinking routines this year, he decides to select only one to focus on at the beginning of the year, since he knows it will take a lot of time for students to master the routines. Rather than teach several poorly, he decides to teach them one at a time using flexible models of skilled performance. He reaches out to the science and English/language arts department chairs, and their discussion reveals a shared goal of introducing students to argumentation before the winter break. They suggest focusing on concept comparison or cause and effect (a weak area on state testing). He

Figure 8 Mr. Miller's Calendar to Present to the Department

First 20 Days 8th grade Civics (example)				
A Turn to your neighbor (TTYN)	B	A Turn to your neighbor (TTYN) protocol Use sentence stems for supporting evidence	B	A Turn to your neighbor (TTYN) protocol Use sentence stems for supporting evidence
B	A TTYN, then join another TTYN pair to form a small group Use sentence stems for supporting evidence Organize binders	B	A TTYN, then join another TTYN pair to form a small group *and* write Use sentence stems for supporting evidence Organize binders	B
A TTYN as part of the Cause and Effect Routine	B	A TTYN, then join another TTYN pair to form a small group *and* write Use sentence stems for supporting evidence using the C&E Routine	B	A TTYN, then join another TTYN pair to form a small group *and* write Use sentence stems for supporting evidence Organize binders
B	A TTYN as part of the Cause and Effect Routine Organize binders	B	A TTYN, then join another TTYN pair to form a small group *and* write Use sentence stems for supporting evidence using the C&E Routine	B

decides to delay teaching the concept comparison routine until the classes are ready for whole group discussion and selects the simpler cause-and-effect routine to focus on initially.

Mr. Miller's partner notes that gradual release of responsibility will be important, so using a shared online document, they slowly build each skill across the calendar. After a week of reflection and discussion, Mr. Miller decides to share his draft calendar with the department (see Figure 8). Although he will tweak it as he goes, he now has a plan to share how he will scaffold students for the year. He thinks sharing this with the department will inspire them to try it themselves.

Work with others to increase the impact of the First 20 Days

In our example Mr. Miller discusses these routines with his department. Planning routines across classrooms is one way to increase the opportunity for students to be successful, since they can compare, contrast, transfer, and generalize the skills.

As noted earlier, we often think students know the routines because we taught them and are now cueing them regularly. For example, if we say, "Turn to your neighbor and share your counterargument," we know we taught "turn to your neighbor," and we just finished drafting a counterargument, so we expect on-task behavior to the assigned peer. When we get social chat across tables from some and complete silence from others, we are frustrated. This is *Groundhog Day* again: We just don't know what days students will be on task and learning!

But let's reframe: As Fisher and Frey said, "They know how to do it, but not for you." We need to make sure we don't move on from teaching a routine when students with larger mental sticky notes master it. Instead, we continue to progress monitor and teach flexible models of skilled performance until students have moved these critical academic, interpersonal, and organizational sequences from their working memory sticky notes to long-term memory.

Introduce routines with low-risk content and situations, then increase the level of risk

In the example of "Turn to your neighbor and share your counterargument," we know we taught "turn to your neighbor," but with a low-risk topic like "share your favorite color." Counterarguments are writing tasks and therefore much higher-order tasks. We need to practice flexible models of skilled performance of "turn to your neighbor"—not just as a physical procedure related to who you're assigned to speak with, but also in terms of how to handle the social and emotional interaction involved in turning and talking to a peer. How do I turn to my partner and share in situations like these?

- What if I don't know this person well, and they don't answer when I turn to them?
- What if they put their head down on their desk or don't have any class materials out?
- What if I don't trust them to be nonjudgmental about my work?

- What if I just heard them say they were going to sneak out to the restroom in a minute, watch a video under their desk, or work on their overdue history homework?
- What if they won't stop giggling and craning their neck and trying to make eye contact with the badly behaved student in the back of the room—do I just act like that weird behavior isn't happening?

If we only taught the turn-to-your-neighbor routine using a simple, low-risk task like sharing a favorite color, our students are unprepared to hold in their mental sticky notes the counterargument task, the social skills related to interacting with another student, and the interpersonal skills related to redirecting or supporting a peer who is less than focused or actively off task. Teachers instead have to model the talk-to-your-neighbor routine using increasingly higher-order thinking skills and riskier tasks.

We support students by demonstrating basic interactional techniques along the way: "To get you and your partner started, turn to your neighbor and do these three steps on the board: Get out your draft counterargument, ask which one wants to go first, then decide and start." This scaffolding supports students in building their skills in developmentally appropriate content and situations.

Communicate routines to administrators as well

Deciding on the right routines, including a visual and mnemonic, and working with others to increase the impact of the First 20 Days are the steps you need to scaffold students' working memory and executive function. Principal Gayle Hines notes that when teachers spend the time building a system of routines, students know how to maneuver in that system. This makes behavior challenges less likely, but when those undesirable behaviors do arise, administrators can reinforce what the teacher planned in the first place.

She says that from an administrative perspective, if routines and procedures are taught well the first time, then retaught to those students who aren't successful the first or second or third time, then there is an administrative expectation with students that "this is it. This is what we do." She notes that it makes conversations easier with students and parents. Since these expectations from the First 20 Days are what the students have been working on in all of their classes, including electives, "there is an expectation that all of Tommy's teachers have, so we just need to make sure that we're helping him be successful. This is what you can do at home. This is what we're doing at school. I think it makes life a lot easier for an administrator from a perspective of, 'I know all my teachers are doing X, Y, and Z, and all students in this grade level are expected to do this.'"

When the First 20 Days are planned, taught, and communicated to administrators, those administrators are able to partner with and support teachers in reinforcing the expectations with a student. "The expectation is all of the students are doing and understanding the same things, so it would be easy for a grade level administrator to go into a classroom and see which students had successfully mastered whatever skill they were being taught during the First 20 Days, and then figure out what they need to do to make sure they get that skill," Hines says. When you share your First 20 Days routines with administrators, they can more easily support you when problem behaviors inevitably arise, leading to your goal of a safe and supportive learning space where students' working memories are scaffolded, but they are also held to grade-level expectations.

Step 4. Progress monitor and scaffold/reteach the routines

Once we plan the First 20 Days, we need to plan how to monitor and track student progress. In Gayle Hines's school, the leadership team provides teachers with roster checklists that help determine when students have become fluent in the routines. Teachers personalize their instruction based on how each class period (and each group of students within a class) is doing.

Figure 9 is an example of Mr. Miller's roster checklist of the First 20 Days routines. This will help him keep track of how his students are doing with the routines and eases the burden on his memory at the same time. We can't always remember who transferred in late, who has been absent on an odd-even schedule, and who quietly opted out of a lesson by putting their head down. Class sizes of 25–30 are standard for many of

Figure 9 Mr. Miller's Roster Checklist

	TTYN	Participate small group	Speak evidence	Write evidence	Organize notebook	Complete C&E Routine	Use C&E routine as evidence
Student 1							
Student 2							
Student 3							

us, and tracking 150+ students requires simple record-keeping such as roster checklists. The data from the roster checklist will help Mr. Miller plan his subsequent lessons and communicate with other teachers in the grade level about their shared students' strong and weak skills.

In addition to our keeping track of student progress, we also want to guide students, whenever feasible, in being responsible for monitoring their own skills. You may want to use your existing learning target or objective of the day routine to monitor this progress. Tools you can use include self-assessment questions, assessment checklists, process portfolios, graphs, and charts to monitor and show progress over time.

In general, progress monitoring encourages learners to do more of what is working and redirects them when they are headed in the wrong direction. People can celebrate their wins and handle their frustrations better when they are in smaller chunks. Big chunks of feedback can feel like overwhelming failure, whereas small chunks are good for learners to reflect on, make adjustments, and grow. Whenever possible, we want to collect and use formative data and give feedback to learners that helps them monitor their own progress effectively so they can become more independent (CAST, 2018). We're working toward independent learners who are internally motivated, as we'll see in the next section.

The struggle is real: Maintaining rigorous goals by using scaffolds

Let's pause for a moment. The message behind *Groundhog Day* was actually that, given enough time, anyone can improve! We are exactly where we should be as long as we hold our students to the expectations and scaffold them to reach meaningful goals rather than replacing those goals with less rigorous ones. It doesn't always feel good, though.

One of the key tenets of UDL is that we should maintain rigorous goals and scaffold our students' ability to reach them, rather than lower the rigor and take from our learners their opportunity to access grade-level standards. This all sounds *so good* until we are faced with a nightmare class of 13-year-olds who can't seem to do anything by themselves and complain constantly while refusing to take out any notebook paper. It's so tempting to just give them a packet of worksheets and keep the room silent. Those worksheets aren't really the grade-level content, but they pacify students who like to fill in the blanks and get an instant grade while whispering with their friends and then taking a nap when they're done. Is that the best they can do?

Don't worry: You're not alone. We've all been there. First, we need to step back and accurately assess the situation, which most of us can't do while we're in the moment. Take a deep breath and ask yourself what routines and structures your students *need the most to get to the grade-level content*. Your answers will tell you what routines to focus on.

The key to maintaining grade-level standards is to slowly roll out the expectations and teach the routines over 20 days (or more) so that students internalize the routines and a lot of student resistance goes away. You have to resist panicking when you look at the pacing guide. Lowering the rigor with worksheets now so that your students are nominally on track with the pacing guide will not help you with higher-order thinking skills and peer interactions later in the year. Yes, it's hard. Just keep going.

Will some students (or entire classes) have setbacks during the year? Yes. We all have really rough days, even with the best routines and structures. Maintain rigorous goals for your students anyhow, accepting that some days will require significant time reinforcing and reteaching the routines, and know that you're not alone in this. By helping your students build fluency in scholarly routines even on their toughest days, you are helping them become the adults who will someday come back to see you and thank you for being the person who cared enough about them to keep them focused and accountable . . . and ultimately helped them learn.

Planning steps to scaffold executive function

- Step 1. Always scaffold working memory.
- Step 2. Decide on critical routines to use across the year.
- Step 3. Plan and teach the First 20 Days routines.
- Step 4. Progress monitor and scaffold/reteach the routines.

As a teacher, think about the following:

- What routines do I have in place?
- When do I teach these routines? How do I teach these routines?
- Are my routines *stable* and unlikely to change? Do I need to adjust them to be more useful in the long term?
- Do my routines help students *chunk* steps into fluent tasks?
- How do I cue students to use stable routines to reduce working memory load?
- What other scaffolds do I have in place to reduce working memory load?
- What action steps do I want to take related to any of these?

As a coach, lead teacher, or administrator, think about the following:

- Are there certain routines that would benefit a specific department (e.g., English, career and technical education) or grade level (e.g., ninth graders new to the building needing specific skills)?
- When do teachers have the opportunity to explore and discuss routines? How can you support this discussion in your current role?

- When do teachers have the opportunity to explore and discuss working memory scaffolds (e.g., visuals, mnemonics)? How can you support this discussion in your current role?

- When is the right time to plan the First 20 Days? How can you support this discussion in your current role?

- What action steps do you want to take to support teachers related to any of these?

What are your next steps?

- Right now, I will . . .
    - send a message to a colleague, mentor, or mentee
    - add a calendar reminder to plan or do a task at the right time
    - include a task in a planning agenda to discuss with others
- Tomorrow, I will . . .
- Next week, I will . . .
- Next month, I will . . .
- Next semester, I will . . .
- Next year, I will . . .

Figure 10 Part 2 Learning Map

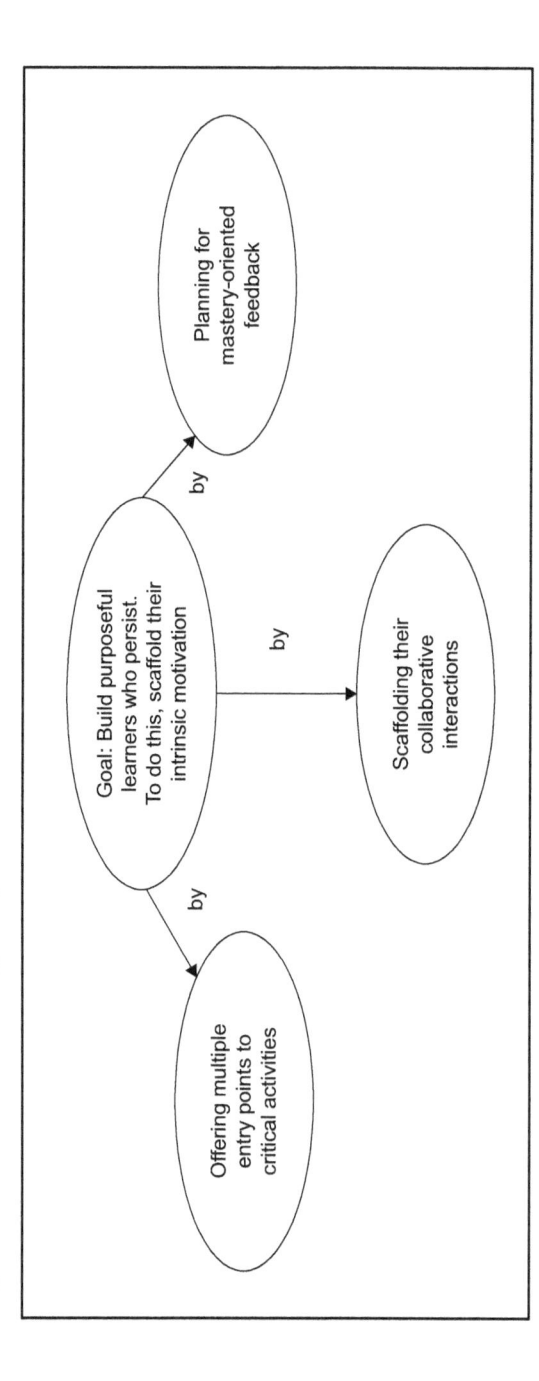

PART 2

Scaffolding Motivation

WHY IS MOTIVATION so important in the middle grades? As we noted in the Introduction, motivation declines in the fifth through ninth grades. At the same time, the brains of students in these grades are very flexible and vulnerable, constantly making and pruning neural connections based on what the students are practicing and experiencing. That's why, despite any innate intelligence, all students benefit from scaffolding.

Supporting students' motivation pays off greatly for us, since internalized motivation is what keeps students going when you step away from them. By scaffolding executive function in Steps 1–4 (outlined in Part 1), we were able to lower cognitive load on working memory and build fluency and automaticity in the routines you determined would make the most impact on learning throughout the year. Scaffolding internalized motivation in Steps 5–7 helps students engage in and complete complex tasks without you having to hold their hands.

Unstructured math tasks, nonfiction text analysis, science labs . . . all of these are complex tasks that go beyond basic routines. Many of us have had tough experiences in which we worked harder than the students to keep them going through a complex task. Hands go up across the room: "What do I do next?" And once again, the teacher is doing the work instead of the student.

For students in Grades 5–9, perhaps the most tempting (and dangerous) practice is to put extrinsic reinforcers in place: "If you complete this task, you can have _____." That's external motivation. At this age, students enjoy and request reinforcers and rewards. These become expensive and lose their effectiveness rapidly, however, and they miss the point of the task: building learner expertise. Middle grade students are in a developmental stage in which we need to help them internalize motivation rather than encourage them to seek external motivators. (A brief note: There is a vast, continually developing field of psychology around motivation. Psychologists have specialized terms for internal and external motivation. For this book, we'll define these terms simply so we can focus on our educational practice.)

The self-talk students engage in and the progress they see themselves make is what helps them become successful learners at this age—not grades, rewards, or recognition. Those external reinforcers don't help with higher-order thinking tasks that require sustained attention and the *try, fail, try again* approach involved in maintaining focus and persistence and making meaningful growth. (Verbal feedback is the exception to the rule: As we will see, it supports the internal self-talk that expert learners use.)

We will focus on a handful of instructional moves as we explore why building internalized motivation is so important, and then apply these strategies to a range of core content. It is interesting to note that in their 2021 book, *Student Learning Communities: A Springboard for Academic and Social Development*, Fisher, Frey, and Almarode highlight the importance of the same pedagogies: tasks, peer interactions, and student dialogue. Engagement in complex tasks is going to be the focus of our work in education for quite some time.

Scenario

To get started, let's join Ms. Taylor as the bell rings for her toughest math 7 class of the day. She has shared with the math coach that this group resists the routines and procedures more than her other classes, and she wonders if she should think about extrinsic motivators and incentives for them.

Ms. Taylor closes her door as the bell rings and steps into her classroom saying, "Good afternoon, class! Touch your ears and take out headphones, phones off and away, binders on your desk. We're working on the Do Now for the next five minutes on the timer, so let's get settled." About half of the class sits without moving, some looking at their phones and others just sitting. Ms. Taylor circulates around the room, praising students who are working on the Do Now task and redirecting students who have not yet begun.

Ms. Taylor bends down to Nevaeh's desk and asks quietly, "Do you know how to get started?"

Nevaeh replies, "I'll do it when I get home." Then she turns away.

Ms. Taylor persists quietly but firmly, "We're going to work on this in class. Get your binder out and I will help you get started."

In response, Nevaeh huffs and pulls her backpack onto her lap. "Fine."

Ms. Taylor stands up and scans the room. Most of the group has gotten their materials out and looks to be getting started. When she looks down, Nevaeh has started the Do Now. Before continuing her walk around the room, Ms. Taylor asks, "Are you good now?"

Nevaeh answers, "I'm doing it, aren't I?"

Ms. Taylor chooses to not respond to this remark, and instead says, "I'm glad you made a good decision," and walks away.

Back at the front of the room, the timer signals the end of the Do Now, and Ms. Taylor reveals the problem solutions and cues students to check their work, then follow their turn-to-your-neighbor routine and share the problem they found the most challenging and why. This activity has been going well with her other classes, but this class mostly sits silent, sneaking their phones out when they can. She circulates and cues students to participate, and as she approaches each pair and repeats the expectation, most students start.

Satisfied that the class is working on the task, Ms. Taylor hands out a sheet for the next activity. Students will be exploring how to mix different purple paint shades from red and blue paint using ratios and proportions. To learn more about the challenges of mixing paint like the hardware stores do, students will read two paragraphs (including charts) independently, think about what is written and what is being asked, turn to their neighbor to process aloud what they read, write two to three questions about the situation, then collaborate with their small group to select four questions that were written by group members and come up with solutions.

Last week, they did this same procedure with a lot of scaffolding, and as Ms. Taylor expected, there were a lot of spectators and several loud criticisms (including from Nevaeh). Students asked repeatedly why they couldn't just do some math problems independently and then work on the computer and listen to music. Several asked why they had to read and asked why they couldn't just keep watching videos like they do at the start of each unit.

Ms. Taylor uses her attention-getting signal to review the learning target for the day, which focuses on explaining one's proportional reasoning. She asks them if they remember the activity structure from last week, and several students nod while others groan and complain about how it was "too much work."

One asks, "Do we get free time if we do this?"

Another chimes in, "Can we listen to our headphones?"

A third says, "Can we have candy?"

This last question starts a lot of discussion among the students. Ms. Taylor knows the teacher across the hall has been giving leftover Halloween candy to this group for completing their work and wonders if it makes sense to have a point system to motivate them to start their tasks. After all, they are reluctant to complete any higher-order thinking, avoid talking to their neighbors about school-appropriate topics, and often ask for games and snacks.

As Ms. Taylor finishes reviewing the directions, she notices that Nevaeh has her hand raised. Ms. Taylor signals, "just a moment" and finishes the directions. She then calls on Nevaeh.

Nevaeh says, "I'm almost done with this, but I don't know how to write the third question. And you won't come over here and help me."

Ms. Taylor thanks her for raising her hand and repeats that this is going to be a partner and group activity, to which Nevaeh responds, "This is stupid. I'll just figure it out for myself since you won't help me."

Ms. Taylor decides to circulate in the room rather than engage in an argument. Her math coach has helped her with *planned ignoring* as a strategy to avoid accidentally reinforcing negative behaviors with attention. Her coach also said that the same way an oven circulates hot air to cook food quickly and evenly, a teacher who circulates keeps her students focused on the lesson and moving quickly through content by interacting evenly with students.

As she reaches Nevaeh's seat during her circulation pattern, she asks softly if Nevaeh knows what she should be doing right now.

Nevaeh responds, "I'm almost done with this, and no thanks to you."

When Ms. Taylor begins to explain the process and group work elements, Nevaeh cuts her off and says, "As long as I get this sheet done, that's all that matters. I'm OK with getting a B from you if you won't help me learn. Can I at least listen to music since I'm going to be done before everyone else?"

Ms. Taylor is teaching a class that sounds familiar to many of us. Now, let's step back and explore what she's experiencing and what her next steps could be. The key is to address students' internalized motivation and how they value and engage in "non-fun" activities.

Building internalized motivation in students

Why do some students take so long to get started, despite knowing the routine? Why are some students resistant to interacting with peers? Why do some students exhibit a general sense of apathy? Since we educators are often alone in our classrooms, we think it's just us: Other people must have this all figured out, or we would have heard more about it!

In the next few steps of our checklist, we're taking on some tough topics: learners and how they decide to act. Will they initiate action when an activity begins, participate in an on-task academic conversation with an assigned peer, and make decisions about how to improve at a complex task?

None of these student actions are in our locus of control as educators: We can't force them to happen. They are, however, in our sphere of influence: We can plan the goal, environment, task, and tool, but even then the learner is the wild card. All the hallway conversations we have about *motivation* come down to this point: We plan curriculum to reduce barriers to participation and increase supports, but we have to engage in reflective cycles to make it happen, and this can be a *very* slow, gradual process. Forget about *students* having grit in the classroom; it's we *teachers* who need it to try, reflect, and try again!

In his book, *Drive: The Surprising Truth About What Motivates Us* (2009), Daniel Pink highlights the need for us to sit up and pay attention to internalized motivation: what it is, why it exists, and what we're doing wrong with people. He reviews three types of drives: biological, extrinsic, and intrinsic. (An important note: we are using the term *internalized* here, as psychologists have technical definitions for *intrinsic* that exclude some of the internal motivation we want to include.)

The first drive is biological and tends to take care of itself: in general, people try to eat when they're hungry and drink when they're thirsty. We get in a lot more trouble when we think about the second drive: external reinforcement. It's often described as carrots (rewards) and sticks (punishments). We have an inaccurate understanding of these and how to use them. School cultures may encourage an external rewards and punishments approach. This pitfall (and the misunderstanding that underlies it) leads us to the final driver: internalized motivation.

Every day, most of us are planning for a 21st century curriculum to prepare 21st century learners for the modern world. Pink argues that extrinsic motivation is the wrong driver for 21st century tasks. It's great for tasks with simple rules, clear goals, and short deadlines: Make an origami crane, or memorize 10 multiplication facts. These narrow tasks can be accomplished with a little bit of focus and thus lend themselves to extrinsic motivators.

But what we really need to do is help our middle grade learners internalize motivation. Why? Because we can't monitor and control people long-term while they do the kinds of tasks modern businesses and academia continue to need. Internalizing motivation helps people motivate themselves because they are making decisions about what to do or not to do to reach a goal (autonomy); it also means that people have developed the tools to improve their own skills and monitor their own performance toward meeting that goal (mastery). When people draw on motivation from inside themselves, the work is more meaningful and relevant because it feels like they are contributing to their immediate community—or even to a larger purpose. That's what engagement and thriving mean in work and in school. Take a look at Figure 11, and then let's dig a little more deeply with some examples.

Autonomy

When we say *autonomy*, we mean learners *internalize* that they can independently make a meaningful decision to reach a goal. When we feel that

Figure 11 Internalized Motivation

> **Intrinsic Motivation = Autonomy + Mastery + Purpose**
>
> *Autonomy*: Learners who believe they have the ability to make meaningful decisions are motivated to think creatively.
>
> *Mastery*: Learners who believe that their personal growth is more important than the reward (or grade) are motivated to improve their skills through learning and practice.
>
> *Purpose*: Learners who believe that they're working toward something bigger than themselves often work hard, produce positive outcomes, and remain engaged. This sense of purpose does not need to be world-changing, but instead can be as simple as believing, "If I didn't show up for class (or work) today, someone would miss me."

our decisions influence outcomes, we are more motivated to try, to persist, and to think creatively. Think for a moment about a faculty activity you were asked to plan. Perhaps you were asked to coordinate the learning at a department or grade-level meeting. It's not your idea of a great time, but you were fine with being volunteered. Someone else provided the topic and a time frame and asked you to come up with an activity.

You may have spent some time thinking about what that activity could be while commuting home that day, then made a list of ideas, and then settled on one to begin planning. You had autonomy related to the activity type, although not the time frame and broad topic. You're now motivated to engage in what we call "level 2 fun": It's got your attention, and although it's not drinking cappuccino in the sunshine, it does reinforce your identity as a professional educator, which feels positive. You are simply motivated to engage in this task. No extra pay or certificates are required.

Now let's think about students who are between 11 and 15 years old. We often fall down the rabbit hole of *choice* when we are thinking about autonomy, and this can be dangerous territory. *Choice* implies an option; *autonomy* means the freedom to act independently to reach a specified goal.

In the previous scenario, Nevaeh may want the *choice* to listen to her headphones and sit on the floor in the hallway while she works on a math worksheet alone and waves to her friends as they travel to the bathroom (we all know students like this). Instead, Ms. Taylor provided her with the *autonomy* to act independently by using time to reflect on the reading, deciding on topics for her questions with her partner, and then contributing to her group in any way Nevaeh saw fit.

In the faculty example, you were not given the choice of timing or topic but instead the autonomy to plan and run the activity as you saw fit. You also were not given the option to plan the activity *only if you wanted to*. This matters because it frames our thinking around task initiation and autonomy. As we noted in the Introduction, we have been experiencing *Groundhog Day* with our middle grade learners for a long time, in part because we expect students to have independent task initiation skills, which are not developmentally appropriate for them right now. If we ask students about choice, they will say they choose not to, or they choose a preferred activity (e.g., listening to music, watching a video, playing a game). As Samantha Layne, an experienced teacher, coach, and professional development leader, points out in Step 6, we need to be consistent and persistent to scaffold student effort toward 21st century skills until they internalize them for themselves.

To maintain our higher-order thinking goals, we need to be careful not to always react with, "Well, why can't they listen to music while they do it? Is there a video of this? Wouldn't it be more engaging and provide more feedback if it were a game?"

The reality is that in the middle grades, just as in professional life, students need to interact with other humans and turn off their music sometimes. They need to practice a skill like annotating text or sketching a diagram rather than watching a video. They need to demonstrate a fluent sequence of tasks like carrying out a lab or building a model rather than clicking answers for a Kahoot! game. This is the *why* behind investing in internal motivation with our students: We can't monitor and control people long-term on the kinds of higher-order thinking tasks the world continues to need. Skills such as responding to a Kahoot!, video watching, and independent worksheet completion are not in demand in the world. Skills such as effective interpersonal communication, complex task analysis, and creative solutions-generating *are* in demand.

Mastery

When we say *mastery*, we mean learners internalize that their personal growth is more important than an extrinsic reward or grade. When we feel that we are growing as a person, we are more likely to try to improve our performance by seeking new information and practicing our skills. In the faculty example, you were given the autonomy to plan and run the activity as you saw fit. Regardless of how interested you might be in the topic, you are likely to be interested in how it goes; after all, it's your activity! You might walk around after you give the directions and listen to your colleagues' discussion or take note of the folks who headed for the door with their cell phones after seeing the handouts on the table. Internally, you are thinking of ways to adjust the activity if you were ever asked to do it again. That's what mastery means: You see the way you can get better at facilitating a task, and you make decisions (some that you are aware of and some that you aren't) about how you might do it differently if you had the chance.

Ms. Taylor also is setting her students up for such a scenario. She has introduced a complex task and has asked students to do it a second time to build their mastery: Read two paragraphs, think for a moment, talk to a neighbor, plan questions, and make a decision with a group. When they participate in this activity, students are using skills they will need in real life, but they are scaffolded so they can practice at their level. So why are students so resistant? Because, as we noted from Dawson and Guare's work on executive function, this is tough stuff—and people continue to grow in these skills *until they are 25 years old* or even far beyond that.

Purpose

When we say *purpose*, we mean learners *internalize* that they're working toward something bigger than themselves and their personal gain. When we feel that we make a difference to others, we often work harder, produce more positive outcomes, and remain engaged for a longer period of time. This sense of purpose does not need to be world-changing, but instead can be as simple as believing, "If I didn't show up for class (or work) today, someone would miss me." Teachers and schools that don't focus on community expectations and routines during the First 20 Days may have difficulty with this later in the year.

Here's an example: When deciding on critical routines, Mr. Smith may decide to focus on personal responsibility for grades, self-editing skills, and make-up work routines, since that is what his end-of-year observations and reflection indicated were students' areas of need. That sounds great, but in October he may realize that each of those focus areas for the First 20 Days reinforced a general belief that students didn't need each other for anything to be successful. Complete the tasks to get the grades, edit on your own or with the teacher, and follow directions to make up work, unless there is direct instruction that day or they have a 1:1 writing conference. Here's the message students received: "I don't need to be in this classroom, and nobody would miss me if I was gone."

This is where the art and science of instructional planning intersect: We reflect on our data as well as predict learners' experiences through *what if?* thought experiments. In this case, Mr. Smith would have benefited from making sure that he met his students' needs not only for autonomy and mastery (with his focus on grades and editing) but also for a deeper purpose through some kind of classroom interaction and community beyond personal gain.

Because of all these variables, it's important to focus on internalized motivation with middle grade learners. We would exhaust ourselves trying to monitor and control them on high-order thinking tasks, and they would resist rather than engage. We can't use personal gain and extrinsic rewards to engage students anymore, since they don't help students build the persistence and resilience required to hang in there during 21st century higher-order thinking tasks.

Why students' *perceived* feelings? Because truth for us as humans is what we perceive it to be, not what it is. We react to what we think is happening, not what is happening. It may be necessary to draw attention to our actions as educators for students to understand what is happening. For example, if a teacher is walking around listening to student talk to decide the next topic for discussion, naming that for the group is better than letting them draw their own conclusions (e.g., "She doesn't trust us and is walking around spying on us! What a micromanager.").

Schools are where educators and their students spend their time: Schools are motivational homes in which we live and grow. Having a connection and purpose in our school helps students—and us—to become more engaged and creates a positive recursive loop ("I belong here, I understand the structures, I can get better when I try, I am part of the group") that gets stronger each cycle.

Supporting students' perceived feelings of autonomy, mastery, and purpose

Although we're anchoring our discussion of internalized motivation in Daniel Pink's reader-friendly explanation of autonomy, mastery, and purpose, we need to pull a few themes from Ryan and Deci's 2017 comprehensive research review, *Self-Determination Theory: Basic Psychological Needs in Motivation, Development, and Wellness*.

We support students' *perceived* feelings of autonomy by:

- making time for students' independent work and encouraging student effort
- giving students an opportunity to talk and listening to their discussion
- offering progress-enabling hints to help students get "unstuck"

We support students' *perceived* feelings of mastery by:

- choosing "Goldilocks" tasks (not too hard, not too easy, just right)
- structuring tasks so students know what to do and how to do it
- providing feedback that moves students forward

We support students' *perceived* feelings of purpose by:

- structuring tasks and interactions to help students contribute positively to the group
- structuring interactions to help students show kindness, helpfulness, and well-meaning toward others

So what's the solution? For students to stay on track even during non-preferred tasks, our middle grade learners need us to support them by:

- offering multiple entry points for activities so students overcome task initiation challenges
- explicitly teaching students how to work with others on academic tasks
- structuring activities around reflecting on feedback to work toward mastery

Unlike Steps 1 through 4, these are not sequential. Read them over and make a decision about which one to try first based on what you know about your students. UDL is about removing obstacles in the curriculum through intentional design, so focus routines on overcoming what students have struggled with in the past. Remember, we're aiming for expert learners who follow the mantra "When the going gets tough, the tough get going." But we often see that when the going gets tough, the hoodie comes up and the head goes on the desk! Choose the step that will best help you break the learned behavior of "hood, head, desk." The first on our checklist is to offer multiple entry points to build engagement.

Step 5. Offer multiple entry points to critical activities

Imagine you've recently experienced a new health issue, and it's weighing heavily on your mind. You aren't motivated to address it, since you're busy with family, work, and other commitments right now—and thinking about a health issue is definitely not a preferred activity. But you have a sense it needs to be handled sooner rather than later. What do you do?

There are *multiple entry points* for you to address your health issue. Sure, you could schedule a doctor's appointment or go to a walk-in clinic, but there are many other ways for you to begin exploring solutions. These may sound familiar:

- look up the health issue online using a symptom checker (always terrifying!)
- discuss it with family or friends

- record your symptoms
- use trial-and-error with remedies/treatments to address your symptoms
- make lists of what you've already tried to address the symptoms
- visit pharmacies or wellness/homeopathic retail stores to explore solutions
- discuss the health issue with other wellness service providers

We're likely to start with one of these, then decide next steps. We eventually address our issues, but we do it *in our own way*. As successful adult learners, we make our own *entry points* to start a task. We may end up in the same place, but our entry points are quite different. How did we learn this? And why does it matter? First let's talk about why it can take a while to find an entry point.

Many of us procrastinate

In addition to noting that our *entry points* to a task may differ from other people's, we need to recognize that *task initiation* can be an enormous struggle for all people, not just middle grade learners.

Humans are remarkably good at procrastinating. We often dislike being reminded of it, but we need to normalize that we all need to set goals, learn, and experience productive struggle, and that many of us just don't enjoy getting started (although we may find satisfaction once we have begun). It's not necessarily that we're lazy, but we may need to learn a new skill, or take a risk in front of others, or do a nonpreferred task, and we just don't feel motivated to do it when there are other activities calling our name.

Our students procrastinate just like adults do. For every adult that is not using their gym membership, there is a student who has still not started that English 9 essay that's due in an hour. Without holding students' hands and doing the work for them, we have to help our learners build their skills to initiate (or *enter*) tasks independently, and be okay with the fact that it's not always fun.

How multiple entry points build internal motivation

Since we know that autonomy, mastery, and purpose are the way to build internalized motivation, we can intentionally plan for it. We support students' *perceived* feelings of autonomy and mastery by intentionally planning a few instructional moves:

- choosing "Goldilocks" tasks (not too hard, not too easy, just right) (Pink, 2009)
- structuring tasks so students know what to do and how to do it
- giving students an opportunity to talk and listening to their discussion
- using advancing questions that help students get "unstuck" (Ryan & Deci, 2017)

All of these are part of UDL Guideline Checkpoint 3.3, provide multiple entry points to a lesson, and help our students become expert learners who are resourceful and knowledgeable about how to initiate their own participation in a task (https://udlguidelines.cast.org/representation/comprehension/processing-visualization).

What does planning multiple entry points look like?

Let's begin our discussion of multiple entry points with a math example. Most of us are familiar with the "warm up, homework review, notes, problem set, independent work, homework" sequence of a traditional math classroom. The order of these steps is easy to build routines around. To build internalized motivation in students to engage and persist in the face of challenges, however, we'll have to do something more than that for students. Mathematical tasks serve that purpose.

Math tasks are problems that focus students on a concept and are used to increase engagement and deeper understanding of ideas (Nyman, 2016; Smith & Sherin, 2019; Van de Walle et al., 2014). Tasks should hook students, challenge them to engage in productive struggle, provide enough structure to minimize the risk of failure, and lead to further engagement.

"A good math task is when you intentionally position students in front of a math problem that allows them to try to solve it through different methods," said math coach and instructional designer Stephanie Burton, noting that math tasks can provide multiple entry points to engagement for students who may not otherwise be intrinsically motivated. She's part of a leadership team that has planned schoolwide professional learning around using math tasks as entry points to build expert learners (S. Burton, personal communication, January 17, 2022).

Math tasks are "the inclusive idea of intentionally collecting what students know, then bringing the whole discussion around to what they know, which is the opposite of what we usually do in math," said Burton. "We say, 'You already know this, so I'm not going to spend any time on it'—curriculum compacting. Instead, highlight that 'the answer is in the room,' and focus on positive reasoning."

Shifting from the traditional math lesson to math tasks is a sea change: It means adjusting our instruction to create an entry point for students as opposed to accommodating the pacing of a packed curriculum. "What an insane thing to do—I don't feel that as a math teacher, I've ever defaulted to highlighting what everybody knew. I just used it to confirm what I wanted them to know, then I moved on," Burton said.

Burton and her colleagues on the leadership team have used examples and experiences to reduce student spectator behavior and increase internalized motivation. "Our teachers were interested in how the math tasks spark student conversation: volleyball versus ping pong," she said. In a *ping-pong* classroom scenario, the teacher asks a question and a single student answers the teacher. In a *volleyball* classroom scenario, the teacher or another student provides a question and students answer both the teacher and one another (Beers & Probst, 2013, 2016; Berger et al., 2014; Berger et al, 2020; Himmele & Himmele, 2017; Lemov, 2021).

Burton continued, "When we shared a transcribed dialogue of a math task in a classroom and math teachers saw how different people entered the topic, they said, 'Look how this student said something about it.' And they were like, 'Oh, that's what you mean by that.'"

In planning the professional learning, she selected examples that showcased a range of entry points. "Some entry points they just never thought about: the context, the topic if you're interested in it, drawing it out, putting it on a number line," she said. "Can students just relate to the situation?"

Tasks should hook students, challenge them to engage in productive struggle, provide enough structure to minimize the risk of failure, and lead to further engagement (Nyman, 2016). Burton and her colleagues have been working on all four of these components.

Hook students

"As a teacher, you plan multiple entry points so they can get a foot in the door," Burton said. She notes that hands-on activities, physically engaging with paper and pencil to draw, and watching a video of a real-life application are all valid entry points to hook students and engage them. "They could be making a connection to something that they're interested in, like science or music and sound or something else. Any of those are entry points!"

Students could be "listening to two students argue over methods, and they are just listening to the reasoning. The student could say, 'I didn't care until the two of you were fighting over this and then I realized, I *don't* think that you're right, but I *do* think that you're right.' That's an entry point," Burton said.

These unexpected moments are actually planned for when we use math tasks. They are the natural, intrinsically motivating learning experiences we want in our classrooms. Students "could be lost or tired or just *over* everyone, but suddenly they are hooked," Burton said. That's engagement.

Although we're focusing on math right now, this applies to science tasks, social studies inquiries, and career and technical education explorations as well. The hook is an entry point and sometimes it's the topic of the task. Burton notes that sometimes the story in a math task is an entry point. Even if it's not a real-life application, if the situation intrigues a student, they will engage with it. "It could be goofy or funny or seasonal or it could just be a topic you like."

Challenge students to engage in productive struggle

What makes tasks interesting and engaging? Keep the level of challenge and cognitive demand high, but let students have some autonomy, as in some choice about the *flavor* of the problem and/or how they present what they are thinking (Nyman, 2016).

Burton says the key to engaging students is picking the right problem, and she notes that we should spend our time "looking for that problem, positioning the students in such a way that it allows for those multiple entry points."

Our first questions include, "What is this math practice I'm trying to teach? What does it look like?" Burton says we have to know what math concept or big idea we want students to engage with and intentionally position students in front of a question with different entry points. Because math tasks require intentional planning, Burton notes that it is important to know what the critical learning outcome is before deciding on the task. Sometimes we have to make up our own tasks instead of selecting premade ones from the internet to ensure students get to the learning outcome. We don't want to invest time and effort into a path that leads to a good, but not important, destination.

But it doesn't have to be a big task, Burton points out. "You could say, 'Here's the number –5. What would be a math statement that I could create with a negative five?' You could then see what they can do with that. You're still getting to practice integers, but the key is the first part of knowing what your target is, what you're getting out of it."

It's important to stay focused and stay simple: don't bite off more than you and your students can chew. "Math tasks highlight the importance of being a mile deep, not a mile wide, so it's the deep dive approach. That is very challenging for teachers because that's not normally how our curriculum is set up," Burton said. There may be several standards or objectives that a teacher wants to address and it's only possible to have students engage deeply into one or two. "But it might just be digging deep into, 'Why does this thing work? Why is this true?'"

Provide enough structure to minimize the risk of failure

Before you begin, you'll put yourselves in their shoes and think about how students might solve the problem, what challenges they might face, and how you will respond to their thinking. This helps you write questions ahead of time to draw students into the task, so you don't have to think on your feet (Smith & Sherin, 2019). You'll use these questions as you circulate and monitor student work in pairs or quads.

Why plan and write questions to ask students? For middle grade learners who struggle to get started (task initiation), teachers often fall into the common instructional traps of (1) suggesting a strategy for students to use or (2) pairing the student with a student who knows how to begin. Yes, both of these approaches give the student something to do, but the result is that you have no information about what they already understand (or misunderstand), and they do nothing to build the student's capacity through productive struggle. It also could contribute to students constructing a personal identity as someone who is not good at and cannot learn this content (Smith & Sherin, 2019). Instead, we need to open up multiple entry points through *assessing* and *advancing* questions we write *ahead of time* to use during instruction.

Why do we need to do this at all? Stephanie Burton offers an insight into the middle grade mind: "Students are used to seeing a multiple-choice problem and the four possible solutions and they naturally go, 'Well, one of those is the answer.' So when we give them math tasks, some students have an internal monologue: 'This isn't word problems. I'm not doing this. I don't understand what's going on. It's too much. I don't believe you when you say, "There's no right answer right now and every answer is worthwhile." You're lying. I know this because there's going to be a right answer in eight minutes. And it won't be mine.'"

How do we address this? Well, we don't avoid math tasks. Instead, we add structure by writing *advancing questions* to help move students' thinking forward toward the goal. Some students have a learned helplessness or spectator approach. They may be waiting us out, or they may be unaccustomed to wading into uncertainty and trying something difficult. Rather than falling into the trap of telling students what to do next, we prepare advancing questions to build on what students currently understand and encourage them to think about something they're not currently thinking about (Smith & Sherin, 2019). It's a nudge in the right direction, but it's scaffolding instead of rescuing. The work stays with the student, where it belongs.

Burton believes a lot depends on persistence and an open mind, which are parts of a growth mindset. "But we know, even as adults, having a growth mindset on a bad day when you're exhausted is hard, because your whole body is responding, 'No. The *last* thing I want to do right now is *risk*.'" We need to provide scaffolds in the form of advancing questions so students get the nudge they need, despite the altogether human reaction of risk aversion.

We write *assessing questions* to draw out students' thinking about a problem or example, so we can see what a student understands or why a student decided to take a particular approach. "Tell me what you are thinking" or "Tell me what you did here" are often good initial assessing questions (Smith & Sherin, 2019). After that, move to more specific questions in which students explain parts of their strategy, so you can determine if they understand the reasoning behind what they are saying and doing.

Spark further engagement

One of the reasons we plan multiple entry points is to maximize student engagement, and our hope is that once students begin, they will keep going because it continues to be engaging. Burton highlights the importance of students realizing that they bring knowledge to the task. She notes that if students can say, "Well, that makes sense, because if that were that, this would be true. Let's try it," then it completely flips it for the student. That's the whole self-efficacy piece, right? So now you have a self-efficacy door." That feeling of self-efficacy can be enough to keep students continuing to put forth effort.

You might think to yourself, "My students can't do any of this." Here's the deal: even if it feels like failure the first time, or even if it feels like it's taking a lot more time than you planned, that time is going to be earned back when students have earned the conceptual understanding that they get after engaging in productive struggle (Smith & Sherin, 2019).

Burton notes that all of us have to have a growth mindset. She has seen the teachers in her school become expert learners as they take risks, incorporate new tasks into their taught curriculum, and adjust those new tasks instead of discarding them when they don't work perfectly. She notes that multiple entry points are key to feeling like a math task is successful, since students have to engage in the task if we took the time to work it into the schedule. Knowing that students were engaged helps us see the value of a higher-order thinking task and makes it seem worthwhile that we took the time for it.

You will see the same thing in the next section on interpersonal collaboration: investing the time pays off. We know this from the First

20 Days, too, since once the students are fluent in a routine, the cognitive load eases and the students are able to function more independently in the classroom.

If we invest time at the beginning, we save time and frustration and students have a better experience later on. This makes sense to our rational brain, but when we're in the moment, rapid pacing can be an intense stressor and influence our decision making. We know that investing in these experiences on the front end takes time and puts us behind our colleagues and the expectations of people outside of our schools (like central office). Building structures that reinforce internalized motivation does take far more time than the reactive structures of extrinsic motivation. But it's worth it to reach 21st century learning goals.

One surprising thing that Burton lifts up is how we discover different entry points: She notes that often, the students come up with them through their natural engagement with a task. You can then plan for them next time. "When you see a student enter a task, you say to yourself, 'Oh, I'm definitely planning that next time!'" Burton said.

As adults, we participate in critical activities through many different entrances, and these multiple entry points are also what our students need to be internally motivated in our critical classroom activities.

Step 6. Scaffold collaborative interactions

In this step, we continue to plan our instruction to support students' effort and persistence by building internalized motivation. In addition to offering multiple entry points so that any student can engage in the activity at any time they are ready, we help students learn to become effective communicators and collaborators in 21st century society.

UDL Guideline 8 includes a specific checkpoint that addresses this: We need to foster collaboration and community (https://udlguidelines.cast.org/engagement/effort-persistence/collaboration-community). How does this fit into internalized motivation? Since students are social beings, they are motivated by positive interactions and unmotivated by negative ones. We must focus on setting up safe and supportive opportunities for them to collaborate positively with peers while experiencing productive struggle. This is an issue for our students who are labeled gifted and in advanced classes as well. In life, they will see other people struggle with tasks and need to collaborate, and they need to experience this as well. Part of the sales pitch on cooperation and collaboration is helping middle grade learners see the need for those two concepts—and the skills they require—in workplace and life situations.

Students who can collaborate effectively learned it from someone

It's important to acknowledge that many students between the ages of 9 and 15 don't have the skills to collaborate and communicate effectively with others. And many of them would be a lot more satisfied in their lives if they did. Although we will always have a range of social interaction preferences among our students (and ourselves), in modern life all learners have to be able to talk and work with others politely and effectively. Like the executive function skills we referred to in Part 1, some students will be working on this through their 20s (and perhaps beyond that).

Students don't learn collaboration without explicit instruction; we just think they do. Our students who are working successfully with others and contributing to a community learned it somewhere. A person took the time to teach it, perhaps intentionally, and the student learned it and internalized it. For the other students, it's our responsibility to teach it. And it's our responsibility to teach it in ways that fit the culture of power in our society: Professional-style collaboration and community are different from some flavors of social collaboration and community. Students may very well be popular, talkative, and social, but they may lack the academic collaborative skills that they need to take a place in professional society. Let's be careful not to confuse the two.

Also, we need to avoid the trap of thinking that children like to be with their peers, so working together will take care of itself. William Golding's *Lord of the Flies* (1954) is a seminal work for many reasons. Reportedly, the author turned to his wife one night after reading an unrealistic story to their children and asked, "Wouldn't it be a good idea if I wrote a book about children on an island, children who behave in the way children *really* would behave?" (Presley, 2017).

As Golding's famous book illustrated, when we don't teach prosocial skills intentionally and explicitly, children and adolescents are left to their own devices and may not learn the skills we desire them to have. Many of us remember negative peer environments from when we were younger; our students can tell us stories of what they are going through right now as well. Instead of this chaos, we use our UDL Guidelines and Checkpoints and plan prosocial student interactions . . . which lead to increased learner engagement and internalized motivation, as we will see.

We need to carefully plan and structure positive peer interactions if we want our learners to internalize the message that peer cooperation is useful and motivating. As educators, we use both heterogeneous and homogeneous groups, depending on the purpose, and flexible models of skilled performance. These are structured, intentional activities, and they are monitored by the teacher to ensure that clear goals are in place and specific actions are occurring. We'll need these elements to create the learning environments for this step.

How being in a collaborative community builds internalized motivation

In his book *Drive: The Surprising Truth About What Motivates Us*, Daniel Pink makes an interesting and important point: Purpose drives motivation, and sometimes that purpose isn't a Mother Teresa–style inspiration that you're helping to make the world a better place. Sometimes it is simply the thought that "My team/class/group needs me to be there today." We have experienced this kind of connection as adults, and it helps us get up and keep going: Other people want, need, and appreciate our presence and our participation. It's not the same for us when they aren't there, and we know it's not the same for them when we aren't there.

We shouldn't underestimate the motivating force of a sense of belonging to a group that is doing meaningful work. This shift in thinking reframes collaboration and communication with others. Working together is *in service of* reaching the goal; the goal is not working with others. It's not a party; it's a purpose.

We need to continually remind students of the purpose of why they are here in the classroom or learning environment: They are a valued member of the learning community. Daniel Pink (2013) notes that exit data from employees who left their companies indicated that those who left didn't feel "I wasn't making a difference in the world," but instead "I wasn't making a contribution to the organization."

We need to assure students that what they are doing makes a difference to the people in the room. This message helps them build intrinsic motivation, which is so important to their ability to be successful and happy in adult life. But, as with any other interpersonal skill, it's too easy to leave it as the *hidden curriculum* of school and of life and not teach it explicitly. As educators, we support students' *perceived* feelings of purpose by:

- structuring tasks and interactions to help students contribute positively to the group
- structuring interactions to help students show kindness, helpfulness, and well-meaning toward others (Ryan & Deci, 2017)

What does fostering collaboration explicitly look like?

Experienced middle and high school science teacher Samantha Layne has worked with colleagues to develop and implement an instructional intervention using a social skills routine called SCORE (see Figure 12).

Students in Layne's school are scheduled for five-week sessions during a daily intervention, remediation, and enrichment "skinny" block (S. Layne, personal communication, February 6, 2022). Who is selected for these sessions? It may surprise you. "It's not only students in the standard classes who benefit from this," Layne notes. Advanced and honors students struggle with working in groups as well, because those students sometimes only want to do the work by themselves. As we think about fostering collaborative skills in our students, we need to be careful not to assume that a students' proficiency in reading and math is a reflection of their proficiency in working with others. If we don't explicitly teach what it looks like to work with other people, we can't expect even advanced students to learn it.

Figure 12 SCORE Skills

> **SCORE Strategy**
> **S**hare ideas
> **C**ompliment others
> **O**ffer help or encouragement
> **R**ecommend changes nicely
> **E**xercise self-control

The SCORE learning strategy helps teachers scaffold students in talking with one another and working together. Layne points out that the strategy even gives students specific language to "Recommend changes nicely," which is the R in SCORE. "Each skill has a cue card that tells the students 'This is how you should look when you're saying this. This is what you should say,'" notes Layne. She spends time practicing this in class with real tasks, so students are able to see the effect on others when they use an effective verbal strategy.

The SCORE strategy also solves one of the age-old problems of collaborative work, which is what to do when one student is doing all of the work and the others are just sitting idle or being off-task. "The strategies we are teaching students in SCORE hold everyone accountable to do their part, so they don't lean on just one to carry the load," Layne says.

How does Layne and her team plan this? They embed the SCORE social skills strategy in a five-week session during their intervention block and call it "Junk Box Wars." Junk Box Wars consists of a small group of 12–16 students engaging in group challenge activities where students are put into groups and given a challenge to complete using materials provided in a box and given a time frame to complete the projects. Projects are then judged and students reflect on the use of their SCORE skills. During the challenge, students have the opportunity to complete or work on at least three different challenges through a five-week intervention period, and then students are able to share their work during a school-wide showcase.

Although the SCORE strategy was created for whole-class instruction, Layne has found that using it in a small group offers the chance for students to get more feedback. "If they don't succeed the first time, they're given feedback and support by the teacher to practice those skills and use them. Then they celebrate the successes that they see," Layne notes. Since this is a learning strategy, she collects data on how students are doing with the strategy and moves all the students to mastery. In whole-class implementation of learning strategies, we often get 70 or 80% of students to mastery and cannot find time to help the rest get the support they need. Because of the small group size, Layne is able to get all of the students to mastery during the intervention. "Because it's a small group setting and there aren't as many students, the teacher can give their attention to every single student," Layne said. There's a quick turnaround—students are given three or four 25-minute sessions to work on a challenge. Feedback is quick and actionable.

There is an element of growth mindset in the SCORE strategy as well. "Not only do they take away a skill that they need beyond their school years, but they have an opportunity to see themselves persist through struggles," Layne said. We often think of growth mindset related to academics, but in life we need to try, fail, and try again in social situations as well.

Similar explicit instruction could occur in any class while students participate in content-specific activities. The important elements are explicit instruction with opportunities for practice with feedback and a focus on mastery (Archer & Hughes, 2011). To move from social interactions as an implicit expectation and a hidden curriculum to explicit expectations and named routines, we have to be explicit and name the routine! We know from our dive into working memory that students do better when actions are chunked into routines, and SCORE is a routine.

We need to determine which students are struggling to collaborate and why. SCORE and Junk Box Wars help students strengthen their executive function skills when interacting with peers, especially task initiation and managing their emotions. "We select students who are unwilling to work with others," says Layne. She notes that, as educators, we sometimes don't set high expectations for our students and don't push our students to develop those skills of working together. Working together is a life skill that students need not only for working in groups in school, but also when they leave school and interact with others and the workforce.

We can determine the collaborative skills to teach and teach them explicitly. In the sessions, Layne talks about how they are working on these skills and they are going to practice them, which will help them to work on their Junk Box Wars challenges. "They're interested in the challenges because the first week we spend learning the skills and they're excited to know what Junk Box Wars is and what the challenges are," Layne notes. When they find out that they have to work in groups, and they can't pick their groups, they get a little hesitant. Layne believes that is where persistence and consistency matter. She gives students positive affirmation such as "Yes, you can do this. We're going to do it together." It's learning by doing. Students may be resistant because they haven't been given the right opportunity, a safe place, or the right environment or circumstances to be successful with learning through doing. But in this place, with these scaffolds, Layne feels students are set up for success.

We can determine the context to teach the collaborative skills, including grouping. "They are doing intentional tasks, are using materials that I feel everyone can be safe with, and are strategically grouped," Layne notes. She groups them purposefully and switches groups as needed to strengthen students' skills.

Once students are purposefully grouped with an interesting task, we must intentionally reflect with students on their use of the collaborative skills. "They don't just come in and go straight to work," Layne notes. She always spends time reviewing SCORE skills, and stresses the importance of *think time*. For example, she might say, "Here are the two SCORE skills that we're going to work on today and that I want you to focus on." Layne then sends them into their groups to apply these two skills, setting a timer as a signal to clean up and put materials away using a routine. When they return to their seats, Layne asks, "How did you do?"

This is reflection time. Without it, students would not be cognizant of their daily growth and the challenges they still have. Remember, every student who knows how to work with others had someone teach them. That instruction was consistent until the student reached mastery, even if neither the adult nor child realized it was happening. Layne agrees: "I'm very passionate about structure and routine and consistency, to the point where I think my students are annoyed by it by the end of the year, which means I've done my job!"

Step 7. Plan for mastery-oriented feedback

The third of the instructional practices to build student internalized motivation to put forth effort and persist in challenging tasks is providing mastery-oriented feedback (UDL Checkpoint 8.4 [https://udlguidelines.cast.org/engagement/effort-persistence/mastery-oriented-feedback]). When we talk about mastery-oriented feedback, we mean that the student is seeing and hearing information on how they are doing and how they are getting better. It's not about the grade ("I got an A") or following directions ("I'm being good today"). This is the feedback we're encouraged to give to build growth mindset and grit: Learners use this feedback to direct their efforts moving forward. Step 7 is focused on keeping students internally motivated to continue learning once they have initiated action.

How mastery-oriented feedback builds internalized motivation

We support students' *perceived* feelings of mastery by:

- structuring tasks so students know what to do and how to do it
- providing feedback that moves students forward (Ryan & Deci, 2017)

Having your students internalize routines and strategies in the First 20 Days is important, since for middle grade learners, getting started on a task is often the toughest part. Once students get started, you can give them *feedback for learning*. In a feedback for learning cycle, you help students see where they are, where they need to be, and how to close the gap. They get small pieces of actionable feedback about how they are mastering the skill they are attempting (e.g., "Keep your eye on the tennis ball and lift your arm a little higher"). This becomes the fuel that keeps them going.

At the beginning of this book, we talked about how important it is to normalize a *try, fail, try again* cycle of learning that underlies the growth mindset of an expert learner. In reality, the cycle looks more like *try, get some feedback on your performance, reflect on that feedback, try again based on what you decided while reflecting, get some more feedback, reflect on that feedback, try again* . . . and repeat until the student reaches mastery.

This is what adults attempt to do, what expert learners do, and what our students in grades 5–9 are doing on the long and slow path to learning. None of this is news, but we need to draw attention to one element: Many students don't have the social and emotional skills to manage the complicated feelings that come with the *try, fail, try again* cycle. We need to be intentional in how we plan learning experiences and cautious in providing mastery-oriented feedback on how students can take their next steps.

It's important to focus on *effort* in the reflection cycle rather than *ability*: Learners who are struggling to master a skill will often say, "I'm not a math/English/athletic person," or "I'm just not good at science/art." This is a deflecting technique and removes the students from their own learning and can seem like a script that students have unintentionally memorized and recited.

Mastery-oriented feedback can help replace those scripts by focusing on one particular step at hand: "You did *x* well and you need to try *y* again. If you do *y* in this way that I am showing you, you will do it better. Go ahead and try it."

We help students accurately locate where they are ("You used all of your coordinating conjunctions perfectly"), where they need to be ("You are on your way to using complete sentences in your writing"), and how to close the gap right now. ("Since you did not have any complete sentences, add in your capital letters and end punctuation right now, just like in this model, and then check each one to see if it is a complete thought. I'll be back so you can show me your work along the way.")

We have to plan for monitored independent work time when we can encourage students to use the feedback . . . and then give more! The success of mastery-oriented feedback lies in seeing it as a *cycle*, and cycles must be repeated. Like the routines of the First 20 Days, we must intentionally plan for feedback cycles so students get used to the feelings related to trying, failing, and trying again with feedback. Although we may wring our hands about pacing and timelines, the payoff from students internalizing the message that even though people don't learn things instantly, expert learners use feedback cycles to improve their own skills is worthwhile. Growth mindset, here we come!

The Socratic Seminar learning protocol that we explore in this chapter is structured for teachers to provide feedback cycles that support students in reaching mastery in planning for and participating in academic discussions. If implemented multiple times, the Socratic Seminar protocol strengthens students' social and emotional skills during discussions, a critical need of many of our middle grade learners.

Teachers who give timely feedback often wear comfortable shoes

When do we find time to implement feedback cycles to move students toward mastery? This is challenging and one of the reasons we saved it for Step 7. If we want students to develop and sustain internal motivation in class, we need to make sure students get usable feedback quickly, before it's time to practice again.

For example, if I sign up for a Saturday morning tennis class for beginners, and I'm practicing swinging my tennis racquet in a parking lot tennis court with 25 other students, I need to hear feedback that I'm doing it right (or constructive feedback on how to improve) at least once per class. Really, I need to hear it *more often* than once per class. And I definitely don't want to wait to hear it until the third week of the class. If that happened, I would not have shown up after the first day!

This is a tough message for us as educators. We have classes of over 25 students who are all working on complex skills, and some have significantly disruptive or disengaged behaviors. The last thing we want to hear is that we need to give more feedback and multiple pieces of feedback each day. It doesn't feel like it's possible most days.

Breaking the plane and active supervision

Why do good teachers wear comfortable shoes? First and foremost, there is a personal practice that needs to be in all teachers' First 20 Days. It's called *breaking the plane* and refers to circulating in the classroom (Lemov, 2021). In PBIS, we refer to this as part of *active supervision* (Missouri Schoolwide PBIS, 2014, 2019). In a nutshell, think of the classroom (or gym, or auditorium) as having an imaginary line dividing where the students are and where the teacher is. Traditionally, it's been the five-foot plane in front of the chalkboard. We need to break the plane in the first five minutes of class the first day and then in each class afterward by walking out into the area where students are and circulating among them.

Students become accustomed to the adult being present in their learning space, giving directions, connecting with them, and providing feedback. It's a major component of positive classroom management and culture. It's called active supervision, too, and there is a relationship between how often you interact with students while doing this and the number of problem behaviors you'll have (Simonsen et al., 2008).

Breaking the plane and active supervision provide the most critical tool we need if we are to offer timely, constructive feedback to move students toward mastery: Circulating in the room to give students feedback on both their perseverance in the face of a difficult task and the targeted skill.

Walking around the room allows us to give *just-in-time feedback* to remind them to use the strategies they have developed in their toolkits ("Remember to use the problem-solving steps of UPSC: understand, plan, solve, check"). If we don't walk around the room and give timely feedback, students receive *comparative feedback* at a later date, like grades or ranking. That's the opposite of what we want to do in building a growth mindset. That delayed feedback can be overwhelming if there is too much at one time, and it often is considered useless by students since the task feels complete and the learning is "over" now.

The answer is to circulate regularly in the classroom (starting in the first week of class) to give specific feedback on where students are, where they need to be, and how to close the gap, preferably one action at a time so students are not overwhelmed.

What does mastery-oriented feedback look like?

What skills do we all need to be able to work in the near future? As more and more routine and easily replicable jobs are being automated, businesses are seeking better oral and written communication skills from their employees for the jobs that remain (Hodge & Lear, 2011). To be successful, our students must learn to problem solve *while* communicating both through dialogue and in writing.

In a study to compare the results of three surveys of top-rated 21st century skills with what is being taught in higher education, Hodge and Lear found that college professors focused on collaboration and critical thinking, but *not* communication skills. Why might this be so? Possibly it's because giving mastery-oriented feedback on communication skills is tough. It may be that those professors just didn't know how to teach it, so they thought to themselves, "Oral communication is a soft skill. I can't teach it; you just have to develop it over time." That's not true. The students who can communicate well right now learned it from someone, and it's our responsibility to teach it to the others as well.

As anyone who has ever hesitated to speak to a stranger, to speak in front of a group, or to give corrective verbal feedback can tell you, oral communication is tied to our social and emotional skills. For that reason, teaching students how to participate in a discussion must be carefully planned. Using UDL as a lens for teaching and learning, we will explore how to plan those steps.

First, we need a clear goal. Second, we need to determine the methods and materials. And last, of course, we need to determine the formative assessment: in this case, mastery-oriented feedback. Let's take a look at how one middle grade educator is helping her students grow their communication skills with a group discussion technique called *Socratic Seminar*. We spoke with Tricia Cook, a middle school ELA teacher, department chair, and peer coach (T. Cook, personal communication, January 17, 2022).

> Socratic Seminar in the ELA [English/language arts] classroom is a teacher's leap of faith that they've set the stage for students to think and communicate about concepts and ideas. It's combining reading, writing, talking, and getting the students to ask open-ended questions to go further into deeper conversations.
>
> We have taken texts from fictional passages, like Renee Watson's *Piecing Me Together,* and they've pulled in and discussed and pulled out more details about the character and

delved deeper into what other characters' motives are and what they think they might be. We've also done nonfiction pieces, where the students have had a variety of articles on topics like microbes and have dived deeper.

Mastery-oriented feedback on preparation for the discussion

Probably one of the things we all do wrong when we use classroom discussion is we don't give enough *think time* for students to get ready. For short interactions, that might need to be 15 seconds, which already feels endless to us, and for longer interactions it might need to be one minute or longer for students to organize their thoughts. But here's a truth: If you just give students a minute to "get your thoughts together" as the wait time, they are likely to get on their phones or start making eyes at other kids. What's the solution? Just like in the First 20 Days, the answer lies in routine that scaffolds student action and reduces the cognitive load on their working memory. We need to teach them *how* to use thinking time and give them reminders of what to think about.

Claudia Bestor (n.d.) has a great example of this in her "Questions Planning Template." Like Tricia Cook, she plans student discussions as multiday learning experiences in which all students are expected to participate. She explicitly prompts students to prepare questions for the discussion and tells them exactly how to formulate those questions:

- be sure your questions are based on the text
- ask questions that are complex and require participants to think beyond what is directly stated in the text
- ask open-ended questions; don't ask YES/NO questions
- ask questions to which there are no right or wrong answers
- regularly ask, "Why?" "How do you know?" and "Why is this important?" to help participants expand their thoughts and responses
- ask questions that require participants to explain their reasoning, their assumptions, and to examine possible misunderstandings

Since students are preparing these questions ahead of time, using this bulleted list to highlight critical features of a good discussion question helps you give mastery-oriented feedback to students (see also UDL Guideline 3.3). You can give verbal feedback in real time as you walk around or written feedback between class sessions; students can then use that feedback to write better questions that will give them more success during the discussion.

Why does this matter? Well, we can't (and don't want to) stop a discussion to say, "Tiffani, your question just now was OK, but it was a yes-or-no question, and it shut down the group. How can you say it in a different way so that others can answer you? Go ahead and think; we'll all wait." But you *could* talk to her the day before and ask, "How do you think your peers will respond to this? OK, how can you open it up so they can say more? Go ahead and revise it! I'll come right back, and you can try it out on me."

These seem like minor instructional moves, but just like in the tennis example, learners need a chance to attend practice and not just the big game. By explicitly teaching the steps to formulating a good question in a discussion, we take oral communication skills out of the hidden curriculum that only some students have access to and move them to the explicit taught curriculum. Students get to see what it looks like to be successful in creating a question and answer in a dialogue, have bullet points to use to critique their attempts, and get to talk it out with a skilled adult or even a peer before "the big game" of the discussion.

Mastery-oriented feedback on participation during the discussion

Tricia Cook started using Socratic Seminar in an inclusive seventh-grade classroom that included many students with disabilities. Starting out, she thought it was too challenging for her students and came to realize that she was the one holding her students back. "When I had the mentality that you never know what your students can do until you let them go and try it, they excelled," Cook shares. She notes that it was "a hard reckoning when I realized I was the one holding my students back because I didn't think they could do that." Since then, she has focused on the skills related to class wide discourse and feels that "the students are taking it further and further."

What inspired this English/language arts teacher to reflect on her practice and revise her approach? "I was a little jealous of the fun things gifted and honors students were doing and I thought, I don't think my students can do that; I wish they could," notes Cook. She found that when she took a risk and planned explicit instruction related to Socratic Seminar, it was successful. Her worries about student skill level were unfounded, in part because she structured the lessons intentionally and as a gradual release of responsibility. "They had a great time, and they wanted to do more," Cook said. Instead of focusing on whether her students could even *try* to engage in the Socratic Seminar routine, she started small and focused on giving them mastery-oriented feedback on how they are participating during the discussion.

As part of the explicit instruction, Cook gave students conversation cues. She also taught them how to write open-ended questions to get deeper into a topic. Like Samantha Layne did with her SCORE and Junk Box Wars groups, Cook planned instruction around how to interact with one another, how to pause and listen, and how to go back to the conversation cues. Those became the initial look-fors to give mastery-oriented feedback on participation.

There were sweet moments along the way. "One of our students made sure a student who didn't like to speak was included in the seminar; they were at first taken aback and concerned and didn't want to say anything, but then they felt comfortable speaking up and thinking out loud," Cook notes. Cook provides a written alternative for students who don't want to speak or who are too shy to speak. These students stay within the circle, are expected to listen to what people are saying, and form their own opinions. Students who participate in a written form have not opted out but receive mastery-oriented feedback related to their participation just like their peers.

The planning process to implement the Socratic Seminar routine is a lengthy one: Cook plans to spend about two or three days getting ready for the first Socratic Seminar. This pays off; since she gives students feedback along the way as they get ready, there are fewer non-participants on the day of the Seminar. To keep things manageable, she recommends starting small and having students read, annotate, and write questions for just one page of a text or informational source.

Cook plans instruction to address the obstacles that can arise, such as feeling uncomfortable asking a question or having to go to the bathroom during the Seminar. Since she starts with a small text, students can learn the process and get feedback along the way without being overwhelmed.

It took encouragement from a colleague for Tricia Cook to address her concerns and plan the Socratic Seminar routine in her inclusive, collaborative English/language arts class. As educators, we don't always talk with one another and build up the support network that encourages us to take risks. Instead, we simply think that our students can't do something. Cook stresses the need to encourage one another to "just do it," noting, "I think some of the reason we hold off on trying things like Socratic Seminar is that we're insular."

Cook recommends just jumping in to find out your students' ability to participate and needs for scaffolding. This "feet on the ground" formative assessment will help you identify what parts of the routine students need more instruction and feedback on.

In her experience, after the first Socratic Seminar, her worry subsided. Like other routines, Socratic Seminar becomes part of the classroom culture. Students reflect on their preparation work and participation immediately after each Seminar ends, not waiting for the teacher's feedback. Cook believes this helps her with implementation.

She stresses the importance of the preparation work as part of the routine: "Once students realize that the prep work helps them to get their brains going," they are more invested in writing their questions and deciding what they want to say during the Seminar. She learned this by watching students and adjusting her instruction. Her mastery-oriented feedback to students focused on how their participation will improve if their advanced planning was more complete. Students who followed that feedback found their participation improved the next time they were in Seminar, and the success inspired them to keep doing what they were doing. "It's nice because the last couple of times, students have really gone back to the text and found examples," Cook said. She has made a question page for students as a scaffold; students can refer to the question page as well as their text during the session. She feels like these revisions to the routine have built students' comfort in the discussion, since they now understand how to not just state their opinion, but also to provide the text evidence to support it.

Socratic Seminar is a complex routine, which relies on higher-order thinking skills. Cook has demonstrated that if you scaffold elements of the task (e.g., text length and depth, content, level) then you can focus students on improving their participation. The scaffolded elements can be released gradually as you think they are ready. Cook reminds us that middle grade students have to think about how to "not get distracted, or upset, or embarrassed, and then talking in front of other people and interrupting at the right time." It's a lot for students to handle. Keeping the Socratic Seminar small to start with, scaffolding their preparation work, and focusing on giving them mastery-oriented feedback on how they are participating during the discussion is a winning instructional move.

Mastery-oriented feedback to reflect on the discussion

Tricia Cook has used a reflection sheet (see Figure 13) to guide her students in reflecting on their actions and setting goals for the next session.

She says it takes time for students to become comfortable speaking and participating:

> Even though we had been running advisory circles, I still had students who didn't want to participate vocally at all, and so they would write reflections. The other students, now they've gone from asking questions, but they'll make maybe a comment. They were very upset if their participation grade wasn't good, and said, "Next time I'm going to ask a question!" And they did. Like they're building those skills up. It's really cute to see them say, "Hey, Sade wants to say something. She's got her hand raised." I love that.

Cook recommends planning carefully so that the reflection happens on the same day as the discussion:

Figure 13 Socratic Seminar Reflection Sheet

Socratic Seminar Reflection

Answer each question using complete sentences.

1. What was your *overall* experience with the seminar?
2. What was the most interesting question?
3. What is one point someone else said that you agreed with?
4. If you changed your opinion during the discussion, what changed it?
5. What was the *best* thing you observed, and why is it notable?
6. What was the *worst* part, and how could it be different next time?
7. What area did you do better with this time and why (text annotation, question writing, participation)?

8. My response to the text:	
This is what I thought about the readings *before*:	This is what I thought *after* the seminar:

Start the year off with seminars knowing you have to teach students skills specific to a seminar. Set the routine of (1) having to read and annotate, (2) writing the open-ended questions, and (3) having the reflection immediately afterward. That was one of the big things that I messed up the first time I did it. We didn't leave enough time for them to reflect. By the next class period, they were like, "What did we do?" Make sure you leave enough time for reflection at the end as closure.

Too often we focus only on the activity and not on mastery-oriented feedback. Pacing is a very real stressor for all of us, but that means that students don't always know how they are doing in the skills that help or prevent them from reaching their goals because there is no time in the schedule for giving feedback to 25 students. Those who have difficulty with organization and planning don't see the big picture and may have a sense of learned helplessness. They need models, guidance, and feedback to see whether they have succeeded or failed, and these examples put us on that road (Meyer et al., 2014).

Much like Samantha Layne's implementation of the SCORE cooperative skills, Tricia Cook's planning for Socratic Seminar privileges the reflection element of the experience: Students don't just participate in the activity for a grade, but they get mastery-oriented feedback to describe where they are, where they need to be, and how to close the gap to reach that goal.

Let's return to our scenario of Ms. Taylor and her class. She asked them if they remembered the activity structure from last week, and some students complained about how it was "too much work" and asked for extrinsic reinforcement. Ms. Taylor wondered whether it might be best to offer candy or rewards to keep them working. We now have three instructional moves to consider as we sit beside her to reflect.

Stephanie Burton might suggest that Ms. Taylor review her activity to ensure that, in addition to the high levels of rigor, there are multiple entry points for students to engage in, and that she has assessing and advancing questions prepared for when she circulates during the activity. Samantha Layne might recommend reviewing the expectations for interpersonal communication and interactions and adding in explicit instruction in any skills that are absent (such as Nevaeh's current inability to work with others). Finally, Tricia Cook might ask what structures could best fit the current classroom routines so that students could see exactly where they are on their question writing, discussion, and reflection skills and get mastery-oriented feedback from themselves and the teacher on a regular basis.

Although Steps 5, 6, and 7 are much more difficult than the first four, they have the potential to make a meaningful impact on both the quality of student learning and your desire to come back to your classroom the next day. In the final section, we'll plan to put all the steps in place in a manageable way.

Planning steps to scaffold motivation

- Step 5. Offer multiple entry points to critical activities.
- Step 6. Scaffold collaborative interactions.
- Step 7. Plan for mastery-oriented feedback.

As a teacher, think about:

- How am I offering multiple entry points for activities so students overcome task initiation challenges?
- How am I explicitly teaching students how to work with others on academic tasks?
- How am I structuring activities so that students reflect on feedback and work toward mastery?
- What action steps do I want to take related to any of these?

As a coach, lead teacher, or administrator, think about:

- In the different content areas, what critical activities need multiple entry points? Are there specific activities the school is focusing on this year?
- What kinds of collaborative interactions cross classrooms and might create the greatest impact if more than one teacher and coach focused on similar skills?
- What professional learning has your school been engaging in related to student feedback?
  - How can you help teachers practice specific verbal and written mastery-oriented feedback?
  - How can you highlight the importance of timeliness and give actionable suggestions to teachers (e.g., circulate in the classroom, and provide just-in-time feedback)?
- What action steps do you want to take to support teachers related to any of these?

What are your next steps?

- Right now, I will . . .
  - Send a message to a colleague, mentor, or mentee
  - Add a calendar reminder to plan or do a task at the right time
  - Include a task in a planning agenda to discuss with others
- Tomorrow, I will . . .
- Next week, I will . . .
- Next month, I will . . .
- Next semester, I will . . .
- Next year, I will . . .

PART 3

Pulling It All Together

THROUGHOUT THE BOOK, we have been using a checklist approach to address a crucial issue: scaffolding our middle grade learners so they can become expert learners. We have explored examples of a handful of critical research-based practices that focus on UDL Guideline 6: Executive Functions, and UDL Guideline 8: Sustaining Effort and Persistence. Through the words of real-life educators, we have seen that this handful of instructional moves form the basis of an instructional model that will scaffold learners at this important and difficult stage of social and emotional development. Now it's time to make a plan and put it all together.

Step 8: Set up and use an instructional calendar

One of the most valuable tools that we all have in planning is the personal instructional calendar (see Figure 14). As administrators, we use calendars to communicate the most important events and tasks to the school. As teachers, we use calendars as a method to make our thinking visible and to make sense of the many competing demands on instructional time.

We recently had a conversation with a coach who exclaimed:

> I always forget to show my teachers how to make an instructional calendar! They think I magically know how to

Figure 14 Sample Instructional Calendar

NOVEMBER				
Monday	Tuesday	Wednesday	Thursday	Friday
Oct 31 B Day Library Day Halloween contest All missing work due by end of day	1 A Day Unit 2 Lesson 9 Portfolios due	2 B Day AM Assembly	3 A Day - End Q1 Unit 3 Lesson 1 Unit Test Projects due	4 B Day - Start Q2
7 Closed No students	8 Professional Learning Day No students Unit test rubric data due	9 A Day Unit 3 Lesson 2 Grades due 8 AM	10 B Day PM Tornado - reschedule lessons	11 A Day Unit 3 Lesson 3 AM Veteran's Day Assembly
14 B Day	15 A Day Unit 3 Lesson 4 Laptop distribution: paper and pencil	16 B Day Laptop distribution: paper and pencil	17 A Day Unit 3 Lesson 5 PM Fire Drill	18 B Day Projects due today
21 A Day Unit 3 Lesson 6	22 B Day Common assessment rubric data due today	23 Closed No students	24 Thanksgiving No students	25 Closed No students
28 A Day Unit 3 Lesson 7	29 B Day	30 A Day Unit 3 Lesson 8	Dec 1 B Day	Dec 2 A Day Unit 3 Lesson 9

pace out units in my head and know that we need to adjust next week since we are losing an odd day for laptop distribution. I need to show them that I saw it in my paper calendar that morning; it's not that there is some trick veteran teachers have for just knowing these things.

Although making an instructional calendar will take an hour or two, and it has to be maintained, most of us have found it to be invaluable in a professional field that requires us to shift and adjust continually. Here's how to begin.

Get a blank paper calendar and a pencil (you will be erasing, so don't use a glossy calendar; use an inexpensive planning calendar like the desk calendars found at office supply stores). It's also fine to type in a document: Download a prefilled calendar template for the year from Google Docs or MS Word. Word-processing applications work better for these than calendars made in spreadsheets, so opt for a doc over a sheet.

In addition, you will need two things that should be available online: (1) your school/division approved calendars, and (2) your school/division pacing and assessment materials.

Large school divisions often have a single set of pacing materials that everyone uses. They may be formatted as tables, charts, calendars, or bulleted lists. Sometimes there are lists of dates and other times there are pacing recommendations (e.g., "allow three weeks for Unit 4").

Small school divisions may have a teacher-created curriculum that is maintained in shared online folders. There may be a calendar from last year that gives the start and end dates for the units as they were taught. Professional learning community (PLC) notes often indicate the end date for a unit, which may be the most accurate date based on the lived experience of teaching the same content last year.

Once you have the necessary materials, here are the basic steps for making an instructional calendar:

1. Using your school and division calendars, mark off holidays, workdays, early release, professional learning, parent conferences, and other noninstructional times.

2. Add the end-of-quarter dates. Add any grading deadlines, and mark the last day for your students to submit work for you to grade each quarter.

3. Using your school and division pacing and assessment materials, add all common assessment dates, including screeners and writing tasks. If assessments occur close to the end of a marking period, move them up as far as possible to allow for absent student makeups and to allow you time to grade after unforeseen events.

4. Add unit start and end dates. For example, if you have eight units, start Unit 1 in the first week of school and Unit 2 in the fourth week of school to finish two units in the first nine weeks. Also allow space for time shifting for unexpected events, like

tornado or hurricane outages. You will move these dates during the year, but you need a draft to start planning. (If a unit crosses a lengthy break, make a decision to extend the unit or adjust the start date.)

5. Add other scheduled events (e.g., class assemblies, picture day, homecoming, laptop distribution) as they are shared by email or the school calendar. You will continue to add these throughout the year, but to start you can look at last year for an idea of when they may occur.

6. If you can, get information on state and district testing dates from last year, and mark them with a question mark, as they may be interruptions to your teaching routines. You will update those dates when the final testing calendars are released.

Next, you'll follow Mr. Miller's path in Part 1 to plan out which First 20 Days routines to prioritize (see Figure 15). If this is your first year in a new content area, use your best judgment to decide on the heavy hitters. Otherwise, use your existing documents and reflections from last year to make decisions that will meet the needs you already identified.

After each break, as Principal Gayle Hines noted, you will facilitate a short version of the First 20 Days as a *ramp-up*. If you teach semester classes, you will run the First 20 Days twice and ramp up students as needed. You can add these to the instructional calendar now.

Each time we return to our instructional calendar, we're engaging in reflective practice. The calendar helps us see the learning context as it really is: what interruptions each student experienced, which broad generalizations we might be making, and where our issues are student-specific versus class-specific.

In addition, the instructional calendar eases the Sunday night stress that comes from not having a big picture view of what students need. Searching online for student activities at the last minute to make sure students have work for the week may undermine the scaffolds we've established with the help of this book. Seeing the big picture on a calendar,

Figure 15 Sample Instructional Calendar for First 20 Days of English 9

Background: It's common to hear teachers express disbelief about the apparent lack of social-emotional skills their students show at the beginning of the year. "They're in ___ grade; they should know how to do this by now!" It's true, and the chances are very good that they know how to engage in partner talk or how to work in a small group. It's likely that they've done these things dozens of times in previous years. But the truth is they don't know how to do it for you . . . yet. The First 20 Days of school is a time when you systematically put into place the procedures on which you will rely throughout the year. In addition, you establish a learning environment centered on personal responsibility, respectful discourse, and collaborative problem solving. After all, learning is really about resolving problems to reach competence.

See page 102 for an example of a calendar of the First 20 Days of school.

- Routine lessons take between 10 and 20 minutes. Do your best to attach them to the content you are teaching.

- The first lesson introduces a skill or procedure. After that, use them *as often as possible* so that students have many opportunities to refine their social interactions and collaborative learning skills.

- Use the Roster Checklists to *track student progress* in the skills.

situated in the units, helps us plan better. We can take things we find online and locate them in the right place on the calendar and adjust them to fit our routines and students.

Remember, the scaffolds build over time, so things we find online, which are stand-alone activities, may create challenges since they don't fit the model of what you've been teaching your students to do. Being able to see a few weeks out helps you plan ahead and lower your stress by planning the right materials with the right supports. That lets you think in chunks and make the pieces fit, instead of planning day by day and hoping that the next day's ideas and internet finds will build on today's challenges and needs.

Routines

Think Pair

Students take approximately one minute to think through a response to a question (Think) proposed by the instructor before turning to partners for discussion (Pair).

Teachers can implement by

- using a prompt, picture, problem, graph
- starting the class with a time for students to think about a meaningful question
- closing a lesson or activity
- using with error analysis problems
- using sentence stems to assist students with starting discussion (I think . . . because . . .).

Organization Set-Up

Student organization allows students to easily retrieve previous work products. The teacher must decide the management system that will be used by students to store and easily retrieve work products (notebooks, binders, interactive notebooks, etc.). Teacher and students work together through the routine. Students understand what materials will be needed and used and what their responsibilities will be (bring to class every day, store in the classroom, etc.). Teachers will be prepared to re-teach when needed.

Think Draw or Write

Students take approximately one minute to think through a response to a question (Think) proposed by the instructor—often one "demanding analysis, evaluation, or synthesis"—before turning to partners for discussion (Pair), collaborative illustration (Draw), or composition (Write).

Would You Rather

A routine that asks students to make a choice between two situations or problems and then justify the choice to a partner using logical reasoning from the prompt, image, or problem. Students think quietly while preparing a reason for their choice based on a prompt. Students then share with a partner (and then possibly with a square). The goal is to have students use accountable talk. Can be used as an opening or closing activity. Can reveal students' prior and current knowledge of a topic. Because there is usually not one correct choice, but relies on intuition and reasoning, it is a lower risk way to promote accountable talk.

Notice and Wonder

A routine that allows students to share their thoughts without the pressure to answer or solve a problem. Students observe a prompt, problem, picture, or text, and are asked what they notice and what they wonder about what they see or read. Students may then share what they notice with a partner, square, or class (without discussion). Students are then asked to share what they wonder. If used with class, record all thoughts and thank students. If using pairs/squares, teachers circulate to listen in to student talk. If students have questions about any notices or wonders they may be asked at the end. This builds self-confidence, reflective skills, and engagement as students discover that the goal is not to be "over and done," but to practice observation, discourse, and reasoning.

Think Pair Square

Think-pair-square builds on partner talk you ask students to engage in throughout the lesson. Use this when posing questions that require more conversation. After partners discuss a question, they join another set of partners to extend their ideas.

Share What Others Said

After using Think-Pair, Notice and Wonder, or another reasoning routine where partners/square talk, allow students to share what their partner said to the

(continued)

class. Up to this point, students have mostly shared with partners or squares and have not shared out to the class. Depending on class makeup, teachers may have students share what their partner said to the square or a smaller group.

Content Specific Text Annotation

Teachers should use the 9 to have students read and annotate a content-specific piece of text. This could be a word problem, chart/graph, play, recipe, passage, or whatever is applicable for that day.

Organization Digital

Teachers use this time to explicitly teach and practice their digital organization. This would include how work is delivered online, how modules are set up, where they can find daily work, any online resources such as digital writing folders or notebooks. This will vary. Please make sure students are explicitly taught how to access the digital materials that they need.

Accountable Talk - Using Text Evidence

Accountable Talk means that students are able to justify their position on a topic using text evidence. Text evidence is discipline specific. This could be from an image, chart, recipe, passage, word problem, error analysis, video clip, etc. Students can use the accountable talk stems and teachers can use the conversation cues to assist in the discourse. This can be done in the whole class or small group, pair, or square. If done in a small group, teachers should circulate to record which students need more support in this area.

Organization - On-Task Partners

This is an instructional move that is cued by the teacher for partners to check to see if their partner is on the right page, or the right track of what is happening in the class. Teachers can prompt using "Check on Partner" or "On-Task Partner Check." This must be explicitly taught and practiced.

In addition, instructional calendars are great tools for members of PLCs. It's tough to look at multiple lesson plans and choose common assessments and instructional strategies to try, reflect on, and improve, but it's easier to look at a calendar and have conversations about high-impact strategies that are worth discussion and a deep dive for all team members.

This is a great time to think about UDL and learner variability. We don't believe that every learner needs their own personalized approach. There are common supports and approaches that are good practice for most students and can be accommodated for the few. The challenge, as we said at the beginning, is that we forget what they are. The checklist manifesto reminds us to isolate the critical elements and requires us to focus attention. The instructional calendar is the deliverable for the checklist. Yes, we agree with the checklist. Yes, we know how to do it. No, we didn't remember or have time. Why? Too many things! Sudden changes! Got it. So we use the instructional calendar to handle those. When we have a two-hour interruption for a tornado warning, we simply adjust the calendar to move the routines to the following day. Yes, this is complex in person, but the calendar is a scaffold for the adult's working memory, too.

As we wrap up, let's acknowledge some lessons learned from the past few years. We know that even with a typical range of learner variability, most of the UDL Guidelines 6 and 8 (see Figure 16) are either within middle grade students' zone of proximal development or beyond it (see also CAST, 2011).

The *Groundhog Day* frustrations we hear from staff arise, in part, from inappropriate expectations that students will be able to independently demonstrate executive function, set and attain goals, and regularly interact appropriately with others for a designated purpose. In fact, our learners are in a training ground for the realities of adulthood, and a handful of instructional strategies will keep them moving along . . . even if it takes until age 25 for most of the executive function skills to finish developing. With our checklist of eight steps, however, we can continue to do the good work that brought us all into the field in the first place.

Figure 16 UDL Guidelines 2.0

Universal Design for Learning Guidelines

I. Provide Multiple Means of Representation

1: Provide options for perception
- 1.1 Offer ways of customizing the display of information
- 1.2 Offer alternatives for auditory information
- 1.3 Offer alternatives for visual information

2: Provide options for language, mathematical expressions, and symbols
- 2.1 Clarify vocabulary and symbols
- 2.2 Clarify syntax and structure
- 2.3 Support decoding of text, mathematical notation, and symbols
- 2.4 Promote understanding across languages
- 2.5 Illustrate through multiple media

3: Provide options for comprehension
- 3.1 Activate or supply background knowledge
- 3.2 Highlight patterns, critical features, big ideas, and relationships
- 3.3 Guide information processing, visualization, and manipulation
- 3.4 Maximize transfer and generalization

Resourceful, knowledgeable learners

II. Provide Multiple Means of Action and Expression

4: Provide options for physical action
- 4.1 Vary the methods for response and navigation
- 4.2 Optimize access to tools and assistive technologies

5: Provide options for expression and communication
- 5.1 Use multiple media for communication
- 5.2 Use multiple tools for construction and composition
- 5.3 Build fluencies with graduated levels of support for practice and performance

6: Provide options for executive functions
- 6.1 Guide appropriate goal-setting
- 6.2 Support planning and strategy development
- 6.3 Facilitate managing information and resources
- 6.4 Enhance capacity for monitoring progress

Strategic, goal-directed learners

III. Provide Multiple Means of Engagement

7: Provide options for recruiting interest
- 7.1 Optimize individual choice and autonomy
- 7.2 Optimize relevance, value, and authenticity
- 7.3 Minimize threats and distractions

8: Provide options for sustaining effort and persistence
- 8.1 Heighten salience of goals and objectives
- 8.2 Vary demands and resources to optimize challenge
- 8.3 Foster collaboration and community
- 8.4 Increase mastery-oriented feedback

9: Provide options for self-regulation
- 9.1 Promote expectations and beliefs that optimize motivation
- 9.2 Facilitate personal coping skills and strategies
- 9.3 Develop self-assessment and reflection

Purposeful, motivated learners

© CAST

© 2011 by CAST. All rights reserved. www.cast.org, www.udlcenter.org
APA Citation: CAST (2011). Universal design for learning guidelines version 2.0. Wakefield, MA: Author.

Planning steps to pull it all together

- Use Step 8 to make your instructional calendar. This is a living document, so take just an hour or two to get it started, and don't worry that it will need to be adjusted. That's part of the process.

- Read over Part 1 to plan Steps 1–4 during the summer, before school starts.

  - Step 1. Always scaffold working memory.

  - Step 2. Decide on critical routines to use across the year.

  - Step 3. Plan and teach the First 20 Days routines.

  - Step 4. Progress monitor and scaffold/reteach the routines.

- Look back at any documents that may help you as you review your critical needs from the past year (e.g., PLC notes, referrals, lesson plans). Use a colleague as a sounding board for each iteration of your routines; consider partnering with others in your department or PLC to make a shared First 20 Days calendar. Update your instructional calendar to include it.

- Make visuals (e.g., posters, checklists, mnemonic handouts) of routines for students. Focus on content and not attractiveness the first year. Are the words on the poster large enough to see from the back of the room? Is the first letter emphasized in the mnemonic? It's okay if they are messy, since you may adjust them before settling on the right routines to scaffold your students. Consider how your posted classroom expectations reinforce the routines (e.g., a written expectation to "follow directions the first time" may help you hold students accountable for attention-getting signals and organization routines).

- During the first month of school, teach the First 20 Days. Use your roster as a checklist to monitor students' progress. Don't worry if you have to adjust; make notes of how to improve on it later this year and next year. Talk to colleagues about how their classes are doing, and adjust if there is something about your instructional delivery that would make a difference in students' learning of the routines. Update your instructional calendar to reflect this.

- Go ahead and extend the First 20 Days past the first month of school if you have a lot of students who are struggling in a class or if you are teaching on an A/B schedule and have only had 10 class sessions. Remember: Go slow to go fast. It will pay off when students have the routines in their long-term memories and can use their working memory to engage in meaningful processing.

- Read over Part 2 to plan Steps 5–7 in the second and third months of school. Before the end of first semester, decide on which of these would make a meaningful difference in your students' engagement in the content.

  - Step 5. Offer multiple entry points to critical activities (if initiation is an issue).

  - Step 6. Scaffold collaborative interactions (if student interaction is an issue).

  - Step 7. Plan for mastery-oriented feedback (if students are not owning their progress).

- Plan to explicitly instruct whichever instructional move you selected from Steps 5–7. Look back at any documents that may help you decide on the focus. Use a colleague as a sounding board. Be sure to make visuals (e.g., posters, checklists, mnemonic handouts) for students. Update your instructional calendar to include the instructional move you selected and how you spaced out the explicit instruction.

- At the end of the first semester, take time to revisit Steps 1–4. We call this a "ramp-up," and it allows you to reinforce skills during lengthy breaks (e.g., Thanksgiving, spring break). Do this as needed when students are in need of support (e.g., testing weeks, snow days). Consider using the daily learning target to focus students on skill development. Update your instructional calendar to include this addition.

As a teacher, think about:

- When is the right time for me to start my instructional calendar?

- How does this fit into my current planning routines? Do I have a plan for reviewing units, and can this be part of it?

- Do I want to do this alone or with a colleague (e.g., co-teacher, PLC member, coach)?

- What action steps do I want to take related to any of these?

As a coach, lead teacher, or administrator, think about:

- How can this instructional planning be part of scheduled professional development?

- Are there specific departments (e.g., math) or grade levels (e.g., sixth-grade team) who would benefit from collaborating?

- When do teachers have the opportunity to plan and discuss an instructional calendar? How can you support this discussion in your current role?

- When do teachers have the opportunity to plan and discuss how these steps fit into existing or potential units of instruction? How can you support this discussion in your current role?

- What action steps do you want to take to support teachers related to any of these?

What are your next steps?

- Right now, I will . . .

    - Send a message to a colleague, mentor, or mentee

    - Add a calendar reminder to plan or do a task at the right time

    - Include a task in a planning agenda to discuss with others

- Tomorrow, I will . . .
- Next week, I will . . .
- Next month, I will . . .
- Next semester, I will . . .
- Next year, I will . . .

Final Note

THESE EIGHT INSTRUCTIONAL MOVES are the right ones for where we are in the world today, but there is more to do. The next steps are to grow where you're planted, which means to invest in your school and start the hard work of making Tier 1 systems change: by grade level, department, or schoolwide.

To do this, we must normalize and hold students accountable for interactions, which we can do through advisory circles. We must set expectations for students to own their own mastery learning, which we can do through learning targets. Finally, we must expect and handle challenges as part of the process, which we can do through expectation plans. These are the next steps of the team of educators behind this book.

Reflective practice is difficult work, as we learned from researching executive function, autonomy, mastery, and purpose, but systems change cannot happen until we engage in it. We look forward to continuing the conversation with you soon.

Acknowledgements

THE INDEFATIGABLE LEADERSHIP of Dr. Gayle Hines and invaluable expertise of Samantha Layne, Tricia Cook, and Stephanie Burton led to this book. Many thanks to Kim Chappell, Kevin Clear, and Kristen Hunter, whose voices will be lifted in future publications. Thanks to Dr. Fran Smith for being the consistent voice of UDL in Virginia; this book would not exist without her. We are also grateful to Shannon Royster for being a catalyst for instructional change, and to instructional coaches Megan Babb, Ann Huffman, Emily Ward, Ashley Clear, and Tiffany Bailey for beginning the innovative instructional model work in the region.

Appendix A

Sample Instructional Calendar for First 20 Days of English 9

AUGUST/SEPTEMBER

Monday	Tuesday	Wednesday	Thursday	Friday
Aug 29 Day 1.1	Aug 30 Day 2	Aug 31 Day 1.2	Sept 1 Day 2	Sept 2 Holiday
1. I am learning to be a scholar 2. It is important for me to learn this because it will help me in life after HS 3. To be able to do this, I must learn and understand Be a Scholar 101 and class expectations 4. I will show I can do this by asking good questions about expectations *Student Activities* - Quick Write - Be a Scholar 101 - Room tour and expectations - Syllabus - About Me inventory - About Me Quilt		1. I am learning to skim text before close reading 2. It is important for me to learn this because skilled readers skim text first to read efficiently 3. To be able to do this, I must learn and understand how to use the THIEVES strategy, what THIEVES stands for, and when to use it 4. I will show I can do this by explaining what THIEVES stands for *Student Activities* - Quick Write (for Binder) - Start Binder Table of Contents - Co-construct Strategic Instruction Model Course Organizer - First Course Q: "We do" THIEVES (Skim Text) verbal rehearsal - Introduce SCORE - Group work: build a tower in trio/quad - Reflect on SCORE and on your group		

SEPTEMBER

Monday	Tuesday	Wednesday	Thursday	Friday
5 Labor Day	6 Day 1.3	7 Day 2	8 Day 1.4	9 Day 2
	1. I am learning to skim text before close reading		1. I am learning to skim text before close reading	
	2. It is important for me to learn this because skilled readers skim text first to read efficiently		2. It is important for me to learn this because skilled readers skim text first to read efficiently	
	3. To be able to do this, I must learn and understand how to use the THIEVES strategy, what THIEVES stands for, and when to use it		3. To be able to do this, I must learn and understand how to use the THIEVES strategy, what THIEVES stands for, and when to use it	
	4. I will show I can do this by using THIEVES to skim a text		4. I will show I can do this by explaining when to use THIEVES	
	Student Activities		*Student Activities*	
	- Quick Write routine with Notice and Wonder routine and Think-Pair routine (no share-use timer)		- Quick Write routine with Would You Rather routine and Think-Pair routine (no share-use timer)	
	- Table of Contents routine for Binder		- Binder Organization	
	- Co-construct Strategic Instruction Model Unit Organizer		- Tracker routine	
	- THIEVES (Skim Nonfiction Text) routine		- THIEVES (Skim Nonfiction Text) routine	
	- Closure Learning Target Tracker		- Using Evidence routines: 3 Big Qs, Signposts, GCDC, and Text Annotation	
			- Patterns of Power Routine 1: FANBOYS	

(continued)

Appendix A | 103

SEPTEMBER

Monday	Tuesday	Wednesday	Thursday	Friday
12 Day 1.5	13 Day 2	14 Day 1.6	15 Day 2	16 Day 1.7
1. I am learning to do close reading		1. I am learning to do close reading		1. I am learning to do close reading
2. It is important for me to learn this because skilled readers make decisions about the claims of nonfiction authors		2. It is important for me to learn this because skilled readers make decisions about the claims of nonfiction authors		2. It is important for me to learn this because skilled readers make decisions about the claims of nonfiction authors
3. To be able to do this, I must learn and understand the 3 Big Questions, text annotation, nonfiction signposts, and GCDC		3. To be able to do this, I must learn and understand the 3 Big Questions, text annotation, nonfiction signposts, and GCDC		3. To be able to do this, I must learn and understand the 3 Big Questions, text annotation, nonfiction signposts, and GCDC
4. I will show I can do this by asking myself the 3 Big Questions as I read		4. I will show I can do this by annotating text		4. I will show I can do this by explaining GCDC
Student Activities		*Student Activities*		*Student Activities*
-Quick Write -THIEVES - Using Evidence routines: 3 Big Qs, Signposts, Text Annotation		-Binder Check -Quick Write -THIEVES - Using Evidence routines: 3 Big Qs, Signposts, Text Annotation		- GCDC with "Blue Light" - Notice and Note Poster analysis

SEPTEMBER

Monday	Tuesday	Wednesday	Thursday	Friday
19 Day 2	20 Day 1.8	21 Day 2	22 Day 1.9	23 Day 2
	1. I am learning to do close reading		1. I am learning to do close reading	
	2. It is important for me to learn this because skilled readers make decisions about the claims of nonfiction authors		2. It is important for me to learn this because skilled readers make decisions about the claims of nonfiction authors	
	3. To be able to do this, I must learn and understand the 3 Big Questions, text annotation, nonfiction signposts, and GCDC		3. To be able to do this, I must learn and understand the 3 Big Questions, text annotation, nonfiction signposts, and GCDC	
	4. I will show I can do this by noting the nonfiction signposts during text annotation		4. I will show I can do this by discussing the nonfiction signposts I noted in my text annotation	
	Student Activities		*Student Activities*	
	- Binder Check for selected students during Quick Write routine with Would You Rather and Think-Pair routine (no share–use timer)		-Binder Check -Quick Write routine	
	- Think Pair Square and Share what others said		- Prep for writing portfolio assessment	
	- Using Evidence routines: 3 Big Qs, signposts, GCDC, and text Annotation			

(continued)

Appendix A | 105

SEPTEMBER

Monday	Tuesday	Wednesday	Thursday	Friday
26 Day 1.10	27 Day 2	28 Day 1.11	29 Day 2	30 Day 1.12
1. I am learning to do close reading		1. I am learning to do close reading		1. I am learning to do close reading
2. It is important for me to learn this because skilled readers make decisions about the claims of nonfiction authors		2. It is important for me to learn this because skilled readers make decisions about the claims of nonfiction authors		2. It is important for me to learn this because skilled readers make decisions about the claims of nonfiction authors
3. To be able to do this, I must learn and understand the 3 Big Questions, text annotation, nonfiction signposts, and GCDC		3. To be able to do this, I must learn and understand the 3 Big Questions, text annotation, nonfiction signposts, and GCDC		3. To be able to do this, I must learn and understand the 3 Big Questions, text annotation, nonfiction signposts, and GCDC
4. I will show I can do this by using the nonfiction signposts as text evidence to answer questions		4. I will show I can do this by remembering the GCDC strategy		4. I will show I can do this by using the GCDC strategy
Student Activities		*Student Activities*		*Student Activities*
-Prep for writing portfolio assessment		- GCDC routine - Using Evidence routines: Accountable Talk routine - Think Pair Square and Share what others said - Patterns of Power Routine 4: Interrupters		- Prep for Socratic Seminar - GCDC routine - Patterns of Power Routine 5: Closers - Prep for writing portfolio assessment

106 | Appendix A

About the Author

Susanne Croasdaile, MEd, PhD, has been a classroom teacher, instructional coach, professional developer, program specialist, systems change consultant, and associate director of curriculum and instruction for public schools in Virginia and Louisiana. With over 25 years of experience in K–12, higher education, and educational research and evaluation, Susanne takes a range of roles to support school-based faculty members as reflective practitioners and to lift their voices to the larger education community.

References

Alloway, T., & Alloway, R. (2015). *What is working memory?* [Video] Sage Publising. YouTube. www.youtube.com/watch?v=TN13Sfyar0U

Archer, A., & Hughes, C. (2011). *Explicit instruction: Effective and efficient teaching.* Guilford Press.

Beers, K., & Probst, R. (2013). *Notice and note: Strategies for close reading.* Heinemann.

Beers, K., & Probst, R. (2016). *Reading nonfiction: Notice and note stances, signposts, and strategies.* Heinemann.

Berger, R., Rugen, L., & Woodfin, L. (2014). *Leaders of their own learning: Transforming schools through student-engaged assessment.* Jossey-Bass.

Berger, R., Strasser, D., & Woodfin, L. (2015). *Management in the active classroom.* EL Education.

Berger, R., Vilen, A., & Woodfin, L. (2020). *Leaders of their own learning companion: New tools and tips for tackling the common challenges of student-engaged assessment.* Jossey-Bass.

Bestor, C. (n.d.). *Socratic seminar: Student-led discussions about literature.* www.elated.us/book-club—socratic-seminar.html

Bulgren, J. (2014). *Teaching cause and effect.* University of Kansas Center for Research on Learning.

Bulgren, J. (2018). *Teaching decision-making.* University of Kansas Center for Research on Learning.

Bulgren, J. (2021). *Teaching cross-curricular argumentation.* University of Kansas Center for Research on Learning.

Bulgren, J., Lenz, K., Deshler, D., & Schumacher, J. (1995). *Concept comparison routine.* Edge Enterprises.

CASEL (2023). What is the CASEL framework?. https://casel.org/fundamentals-of-sel/what-is-the-casel-framework

CAST (2011). *Universal design for learning guidelines version 2.0 [graphic organizer].* Author.

CAST (2018). Checkpoint 6.4: Enhance capacity for monitoring progress. *Universal design for learning guidelines version 2.2.* https://udlguidelines.cast.org/action-expression/executive-functions

/monitoring-progress/monitoring-progress

Dawson, P., & Guare, R. (2012). *Coaching students with executive skills deficits*. Guilford Press.

Dawson, P., & Guare, R. (2018). *Executive skills in children and adolescents: A practical guide to assessment and intervention*. Guilford Press.

Delpit, L. (1988). The silenced dialogue: Power and pedagogy in educating other people's children. *Harvard Educational Review, 58*(3), 280–298.

Deshler, D., & Lenz, K. (2004). *Teaching content to all: Evidence-based inclusive practices in middle and secondary schools*. Pearson.

Doherty, T. A., Barker, L. A., Denniss, R., Jalil, A., & Beer, M. D. (2015). The cooking task: Making a meal of executive functions. *Frontiers in Behavioral Neuroscience, 9*, 22. https://doi.org/10.3389/fnbeh.2015.00022

Doolittle, P. (2013). [Video] TED. How your "working memory" makes sense of the world [Video]. YouTube. www.youtube.com/watch?v=UWKvpFZJwcE

Elliott, J., Gathercole, S., Alloway, T., Holmes, J., & Kirkwood, H. (2010). An evaluation of a classroom-based intervention to help overcome working memory difficulties and improve long-term academic achievement. *Journal of Cognitive Education and Psychology, 9*(3), 227–250. https://doi.org/10.1891/1945-8959.9.3.227

Fisher, D., & Frey, N. (2011). *Engaging the adolescent learner: The first 20 days establishing productive group work in the classroom*. International Reading Association.

Fisher, D., & Frey, N. (2021). *Better learning through structured teaching: A framework for the gradual release of responsibility* (3rd ed.). ASCD.

Fisher, D., Frey, N., & Almarode, J. (2021). *Student learning communities: A springboard for academic and social development*. ASCD.

Gathercole, S., & Alloway, T. (2007). *Understanding working memory: A classroom guide*. Harcourt Assessment.

Gathercole, S., Alloway, T., Kirkwood, H., Elliott, J., Holmes, J., & Hilton, K. (2008). Attentional and executive function behaviours in children with poor working memory. *Learning and Individual Differences, 18*(2), 214–223. https://doi.org/10.1016/j.lindif.2007.10.003

Gathercole, S., Woolgar, F., Kievit, R., Astle, D., Manly, T., Holmes, J., & CALM Team (2016). How common are WM deficits in children with difficulties in reading and mathematics? *Journal of Applied Research in Memory and Cognition, 5*(4), 384–394. https://doi.org/10.1016/j.jarmac.2016.07.013

Gawande, A. (2009). *The checklist manifesto: How to get things right*. Metropolitan Books.

Gillet, N., Vallerand, R., & Lafrenière, M. (2012). Intrinsic and extrinsic school motivation as a function of age: The mediating role of autonomy support. *Social Psychology of Education: An International Journal, 15*(1), 77–95. https://doi.org/10.1007/s11218-011-9170-2

Gladwell, M. (2008). *Outliers: The Story of Success*. Little, Brown.

Gnambs, T., & Hanfstingl, B. (2016). The decline of academic motivation during adolescence: An accelerated longitudinal cohort analysis on the effect of psychological need satisfaction. *Educational Psychology, 36*, 1698–1712. https://doi:10.1080/01443410.2015.1113236

Goodwin, B., Rouleau, K., & Gibson, T. (2020). *Learning that sticks: A brain-based model for K-12 instructional design and delivery.* ASCD.

Goodwin, B., Rouleau, K., Abla, C., Baptiste, K., Gibson, T., & Kimball, M. (2023). *The new classroom instruction that works: The best research-based strategies for increasing student achievement.* ASCD.

Hale, M., & City, E. (2002). "But how do you do that?": Decision making for the seminar facilitator. In Holden, J., & Schmit, J. (eds.), *Inquiry and the literary text: Constructing discussions in the English classroom.* NCTE.

Hawley, D. (2021). How old do you have to be to rent a car? JD Power. www.jdpower.com/cars/shopping-guides/how-old-do-you-have-to-be-to-rent-a-car

Himmele, P., & Himmele, W. (2017). *Total participation techniques: Making every student an active learner.* ASCD.

Hodge, K., & Lear, J. (2011). Employment skills for 21st century workplace: The gap between faculty and student perceptions. *Journal of Career and Technical Education, 26*(2). http://doi.org/10.21061/jcte.v26i2.523

Holmes, J. (2018). Working memory and classroom learning [Video] Cambridge University Press ELT. YouTube. www.youtube.com/watch?v=WUxo5s8HHcE

Lemov, D. (2021). *Teach like a champion 3.0: 63 techniques that put students on the path to college* (3rd ed.). Jossey-Bass.

Lepper, M., Corpus, J., & Iyengar, S. (2005). Intrinsic and extrinsic motivational orientations in the classroom: Age differences and academic correlates. *Journal of Educational Psychology, 97*(2), 184–196. https://doi.org/10.1037/0022-0663.97.2.184

Linder, R. (2014). *Chart sense: Common sense charts to teach 3–8 informational text and literature.* The Literacy Initiative.

Linder, R. (2015). *Chart sense for writing: Over 70 common sense charts with tips and strategies to teach 3–8 writing.* The Literacy Initiative.

Marzano, R., Pickering, D., & Pollock, J. (2001). *Classroom instruction that works: Research-based strategies for increasing student achievement.* ASCD.

Medic, G., Wille, M., & Hemels, M. (2017). Short- and long-term health consequences of sleep disruption. *Nature and Science of Sleep, 9*, 151–161.

Meyer, A., Rose, D., & Gordon, D. (2014). *Universal design for learning: Theory and practice.* CAST.

Michaels, S., O'Connor, M., Williams Hall, M., & Resnick, L. (2016). *Accountable Talk® sourcebook: For classroom conversation that works.* University of Pittsburgh Institute for Learning.

Missouri Schoolwide PBIS. (2014). MO SW-PBS teacher tool: Active supervision. https://pbismissouri.org/wp-content/uploads/2017/06/ECP5.1-Teacher-Tool-Classroom-Active-Supervision-1.pdf

Missouri Schoolwide PBIS. (2019). *Missouri schoolwide positive behavior* support handbook. https://pbismissouri.org/wp-content/uploads/2021/03/1.-MO-SW-PBS-Handbook-2019-2020-V2.pdf

Moser, C., Schoenebeck, S., & Resnick, P. (2019). Impulse buying: Design practices and consumer needs. In *CHI Conference on Human Factors in Computing Systems Proceedings*. ACM CHI. https://doi.org/10.1145/3290605.3300472

Nyman, R. (2016). What makes a mathematical task interesting? *Educational Research and Reviews, 11*(16), 1509–1520. https://doi.org/10.5897/ERR2016.2919

Pink, D. (2009). *Drive: The surprising truth about what motivates us*. Penguin.

Pink, D. (2013). *Purpose: Why we do what we do* [Conference presentation]. REACH Conference. [Video.] YouTube. www.youtube.com/watch?v=_p4esMj2EC8

Presley, N. (June 2017). Lord of the Flies and The Coral Island. William Golding Official Site. https://william-golding.co.uk/lord-flies-coral-island

Ramis, H. (Director). (1993). *Groundhog Day* [Film]. Columbia Pictures.

Ryan, R., & Deci, E. (2017). *Self-determination theory: Basic psychological needs in motivation, development, and wellness*. Guilford Press.

Simonsen, B., Fairbanks, S., Briesch, A., Myers, D., & Sugai, G. (2008). Evidence-based practices in classroom management: Consideration for research to practice. *Education and Treatment of Children, 31*(3), 351–380. https://dropoutprevention.org/wp-content/uploads/2015/05/Simonsen_Fairbanks_Briesch_Myers_Sugai_2008.pdf

Smith, M., & Sherin, M. (2019). *The five practices in practice: Successfully orchestrating mathematics discussions in your middle school math classroom*. Corwin.

Tomm, T. (2022). Junk box wars. The Science Spot. https://sciencespot.net/Pages/junkbox.html

Van de Walle, J., Bay-Williams, J., & Lovin, L. (2014). *Teaching student-centered mathematics: Developmentally-appropriate instruction for grades 6–8*. Pearson.

Vernon, D., Schumaker, J., & Deshler, D. (1993). *SCORE skills: Social skills for cooperative groups*. Edge Enterprises.

Index

accountability
   of middle schools, xii
   of professionals, checklists in, 5
   of students, 39, 65–66, 93, 97
accountable talk routine, 33, 89, 90, 106fig
active supervision, 71–72
administrators, communication of First 20 Days routines to, 36–37
advancing questions, 60
Alloway, R., 21
Alloway, T., 21, 28
Almarode, J., 44
Annotation Poster, 90
Archer, A., 7, 67
argument construction
   counterargument tasks in, 35–36
   First 20 Days routines on, 32, 32fig, 33, 33fig, 35
assessing questions, 60, 61
attention
   scaffolding of, 17
   sustained, 22, 23
attention-deficit disorder, 25
automaticity, 25, 43
autonomy, perceived feelings of
   and choice, 49, 50
   definition of, 48
   and motivation, 48–50, 51, 53, 56
   in multiple entry points, 56
   and purpose, 52

barriers to student success, 8–11. *See also* obstacles and barriers to student success
Beers, K., 57
Bellringer, 14, 15, 29
Berger, R., 29, 57
Bestor, Claudia, 74
binder checks
   instructional calendar on, 105fig
   teacher circulation for, 15–16, 17
binder organization routines, 28, 29, 34fig, 103fig
brain
   plasticity of, 21, 43
   in repetitive practice of disengagement, 21
brainstorming on First 20 Days routines, 32, 32fig
breaking the plane, 71–72
Bulgren, J., 32
Burton, Stephanie, xiii, 56–62, 80

CAST, 3, 9, 38, 91, 92
cause-and-effect analysis in First 20 Days, 32fig, 33fig, 34, 34fig
Chart Sense (Linder), 30

The Checklist Manifesto: How to Get Things Right (Gawande), 5
checklists
    for addressing obstacles and developing expert learners, 10–11
    importance for instructional models, 4–8
    on instructional practices, 5, 5fig
    in progress monitoring, 37–38, 38fig
    supporting student time-management skills, 3
choice, and autonomy, 49, 50
chunking activities, 11, 17, 18, 26–27
circulation of teachers in classroom
    breaking the plane and active supervision in, 71–72
    mastery-oriented feedback in, 74–75
    in math instruction, 45, 46
    planned ignoring in, 46
    progress monitoring in, 14
    student perceptions on, 52
    in THIEVES routine, 17
classroom discussions, 73–80
    participation in, 75–78
    preparation for, 73–75
    reflection on, 77–80
    in Socratic Seminar, 71, 73–74, 75–80
Classroom Instruction That Works (Marzano), xi, 4
cognitive load, 21, 43
    routines reducing, 32, 61–62, 74
collaborative interactions, 62–69
    explicit teaching on, 54, 62–66, 67–68
    instructional calendar on, 94
    instructional practices checklist on, 5fig
    in Junk Box Wars, 66, 67–68
    learning map on, 42fig
    purpose in, 63–65
    resistance of students to, 67–68
    routines in, 28, 29
    scaffolding of, 62–69, 80–81
    SCORE strategy on, 29, 64–69, 79–80
    social and professional, comparison of, 63–64
    UDL Guidelines on, 62–63, 64
communication
    with administrators on First 20 Days routines, 36–37
    in classroom discussions, 73–80
    in collaborative interactions, 28, 29, 62–69
    explicit instruction on skills in, 74–76
    in First 20 Days, 32, 32fig, 33, 33fig, 35–36
    mastery-oriented feedback on, 72–73, 73–80
    in Socratic Seminar, 71, 73–74, 76–80
    in turn to your neighbor routines, 31, 34fig, 35–36, 45
complex and multistep tasks
    chunking of, 26
    motivation and engagement in, 43, 44, 50, 51
    persistence of independent learners in, 3
    routines in, 30
    in start-of-class, 13–19
    working memory in, 19–21, 24–25, 26
compliance behaviors, 6
    coronavirus pandemic affecting, 8
    and resistance. *See* resistance of students
Cook, Tricia, xiii, 73, 75–80
cooking tasks, executive function in, 19, 20fig, 27
coronavirus pandemic, 7–10, 31
counterargument tasks, 35–36
COVID pandemic, 7–10, 31
critical activities, multiple entry points in, 54–62. *See also* multiple entry points in critical activities
critical routines in scaffolding executive function, 28–30, 40
    instructional practices checklist on, 5fig
    learning map on, 12fig
culture of power, 10, 63–64

curriculum
	explicit instruction of. *See* explicit instruction
	goals of, 3–4
	hidden, 6, 10, 67–68, 74–75

Dawson, P., 9, 21, 23, 51
Deci, E., 53, 56, 65, 69
decision making, autonomy and choice in, 48–49, 50
deep dive approach, 59
Delpit, Lisa, 10
Deshler, D., 30
digital organization, 90
discussions in classroom. *See* classroom discussions
disengagement, repetitive practice of, 22
Doherty, T. A., 19
Doolittle, P., 20
Drive: The Surprising Truth About What Motivates Us (Pink), 47–48, 64
drives, and motivation, 47–48

Elliott, J., 28
engagement of students
	checklist approach for, 5
	in complex tasks, 44
	coronavirus pandemic affecting, 8
	in math instruction, 44–47, 56–61
	in multiple entry points, 56, 61–62
	in nonpreferred tasks, 47, 54, 55
	in productive struggle, 56, 58–59, 61, 62, 62–63
	and repetitive practice of disengagement, 22
	and resistance, 47, 51
English language learners, 25, 26, 33
entry points, multiple, in critical activities, 54–62. *See also* multiple entry points in critical activities
evidence-based arguments constructed by students, 32, 32fig, 33fig
evidence-based practices, 4
executive function, 13–41
	in cooking tasks, 19, 20fig, 27
	in critical routines, 5fig, 12fig, 28–30, 40
	definition of, 13, 19
	in First 20 Days routines, 5fig, 11, 12fig, 30–37, 40, 41
	instructional practices checklist on, 5fig
	learning map on, 12fig
	long-term scaffolding of, 9–10
	maintaining rigorous goals for, 38–39
	mnemonics for scaffolding, 30
	planning steps for scaffolding, 40–41
	progress monitoring and reteaching of, 5fig, 12fig, 35, 37–39, 40
	skills in, 22, 23
	verbal rehearsal of routines for, 28
	visual resources for scaffolding, 30
	working memory in, 4, 5fig, 11, 12fig, 24, 25–28, 40, 41
expert learners, 2
	checklists in development of, 10–11
	executive function and working memory of, 21, 24
	UDL Guidelines on, 3
explicit instruction
	on collaborative interactions, 54, 62–66, 67–68
	on communication skills, 74–76
	compared to hidden curriculum, 6, 10, 67–68
external motivation, 46
	limitations of, 43–44, 48, 52
	rewards and punishment in, 48

failure
	multiple entry points minimizing risk of, 56, 59–61
	in try, fail, try again cycle. *See* try, fail, try again cycle
feedback
	comparative, 72
	delayed, 71–73
	in First 20 Days, 70
	formative, 4
	just-in-time, 71–73, 82
	for learning, 69–70

feedback (cont.)
   mastery-oriented. *See* mastery-oriented feedback
   in progress monitoring, 38
   in try, fail, try again cycle, 69–70
First 20 Days routines, 11, 30–37, 40, 41
   across-classroom planning on, 33–34
   administrator support of, 36–37
   brainstorming on, 32, 32fig
   breaking the plane in, 71–72
   cognitive load in, 61–62
   feedback on, 71
   Fisher and Frey on, 6
   fluency in, 62
   instructional calendar on, 34, 34fig, 86–87, 87fig, 93–94, 102fig
   instructional practices checklist on, 5fig
   investing time in, 61–62
   learning map on, 12fig
   low-risk tasks in, 35–36
   mastery-oriented feedback in, 69–70
   perceived feelings of purpose in, 51–52
   progress monitoring on, 37–38, 38fig
   ramp-up in, 86
   reflection on, 31–34
   roster checklist on, 37–38, 38fig
   student–teacher relationships in, 31
Fisher, D., 6, 8, 27, 35, 44
Frey, N., 6, 8, 27, 35, 44

Gathercole, S., 21, 28
Gawande, Atul, 5
GCDC routines in instructional calendar, 105fig
Gillet, N., 1
Gladwell, Malcolm, xii
Gnambs, T., 1
goals
   autonomy in decisions on, 48–49
   of curriculum, 3–4
   and executive function, 19, 20fig, 24–25
   learner variability in, 25
"Goldilocks" tasks, 53, 56

Golding, William, 63–64
Goodwin, B., 4
grade-level content, routines and structures for, 39
gradual release of responsibility, 3, 8, 9, 10
   in First 20 Days, 34
   in Socratic Seminar, 75–76, 77–78
Groundhog Day (film), 6, 7, 27, 35, 38, 50, 91
growth mindset
   Burton on, 60, 61
   of expert learners, 70
   of independent learners, 3
   of lifelong learners, 4
   in mastery-oriented feedback, 69–72, 73–74
   in SCORE strategy, 66–67
   in try, fail, try again cycle, 4, 69–70
Guare, R, 9, 21, 23, 51

habits, 21
Hanfstingl, B., 1
Hawley, D, 9
helplessness, learned, 60, 79–80
hidden curriculum, 6, 10, 67–68, 74–75
Himmele, P., 29, 57
Himmele, W., 29, 57
Hines, Gayle, xii–xiii, 30–31, 36–37, 86
Hodge, K., 73
Holmes, J., 26
Hughes, C., 7, 67

independent learners, 1, 3
instructional calendars, 11, 83–96
   examples of, 34fig, 84fig, 105fig
   on First 20 Days, 34, 34fig, 86, 87fig, 93–94, 105fig
   instructional practices checklist on, 5fig
   steps in preparation of, 83–87, 93
instructional models, xi
   importance of checklists for, 4–8
   UDL framework in, xiii, 5, 9
intelligence quotient, 21

interpersonal behaviors, 6, 7–8, 9
intrinsic motivation, 43–81. *See also* motivation

Junk Box Wars, 66–67, 76

Layne, Samantha, xiii, 50, 64–69, 76, 80
Lear, J., 73
learned helplessness, 60, 79–80
learner variability, 91
 in goals, 25
 in working memory, 22–23
learning maps
 on executive function, 12fig
 on motivation, 42fig
learning routines, 28, 29
Lemov, D., 29, 57, 71
Lenz, K., 30
Lepper, M., 1
Linder, R., 30
long-term memory, 27, 32, 35
Lord of the Flies (Golding), 63–64

Management in the Active Classroom (Berger), 29
Marzano, R., xi, 4
mastery, perceived feelings of
 definition of, 50
 feedback supporting, 69–80
 and motivation, 48, 49fig, 50–51, 53, 56, 69–80
 in multiple entry points, 56
 and purpose, 52
 scripts affecting, 69–70
 in try, fail, try again cycle, 69–70
mastery-oriented feedback, 54, 69–80
 in breaking the plane and active supervision, 71–72
 growth mindset in, 69–72,
 instructional calendar on, 94
 instructional practices checklist on, 5fig
 learning map on, 42fig
 multiple cycles of, 70–72
 planning for, 69–80
 on preparation for discussions, 73–75
 in Socratic Seminar, 71, 73–74, 75–80
 in try, fail, try again cycle, 69–71
 UDL Guidelines on, 69, 74
math instruction, 44–47, 49–50
 multiple entry points in, 56–61
 resistance of students in, 44–47, 51, 60
memory
 long-term, 27, 32, 35
 short-term, 27
 working. *See* working memory
metacognition, 23
Meyer, A., 21, 80
Michaels, S., 33
Missouri Schoolwide PBIS, 6, 71–72
mnemonics, 30
 THIEVES, 17, 18fig, 102fig, 103fig
modeling of talk-to-your-neighbor in riskier tasks, 36
Moser, C., 9
motivation, 1, 11, 43–81
 autonomy in, 48–50, 51, 53, 56
 in collaborative interactions, 5fig, 42fig, 54, 62–69, 80–81
 decline in, 1, 43
 drives in, 47–48
 external, 43–44, 46, 48, 52
 hook for students in, 56, 58
 instructional practices checklist on, 5fig
 learning map on, 42fig
 mastery in, 48, 49fig, 50–51, 53, 56, 69–80
 in math instruction, 44–47, 49–50, 56–61
 in multiple entry points to critical activities, 5fig, 11, 42fig, 54–62, 80–81
 in nonpreferred tasks, 47, 54, 55
 and procrastination, 55
 purpose in, 48, 49fig, 51–53, 56, 63–65
multiple entry points in critical activities, 11, 54–62, 80–81
 assessing and advancing questions prepared for, 60–61

Index | 117

multiple entry points in critical activities (cont.)
    autonomy in, 56
    challenge of productive struggle in, 56, 58–59
    engagement in, 56, 61–62
    as hook for students, 56, 58
    instructional calendar on, 94
    instructional practices checklist on, 5fig
    learning map on, 42fig
    minimizing risk of failure in, 56, 59–61
    planning for, 56–62
    UDL Guidelines on, 56
multistep tasks. *See* complex and multistep tasks
multi-tiered systems of supports (MTSS), 5–6

The New Classroom Instruction That Works (Goodwin), 4
nonpreferred tasks, motivation in, 47, 54, 55
Notice and Note strategy, 29, 104fig
Notice and Wonder routine, 89, 103fig
Nyman, R., 56, 58

obstacles and barriers to student success, 8–11
    checklist approach to, 10–11
    intentional design in removal of, 54
    sleep deprivation as, 8–9
On-Task Partner Check, 90
organization
    of binders, 28, 29, 34fig, 102fig, 103fig
    definition of, 23
    digital, 90
    as executive function skill, 23, 24
    in First 20 Days, 32, 32fig, 33fig, 34fig
    routines in, 28, 29, 88
Outliers (Gladwell), xii

Patterns of Power Routine, 103fig, 105fig
PBIS (positive behavior interventions and supports), 5–6, 71–72
PBS (positive behavior support), xi, 5
peer interactions, 28, 29
    collaborative, 62–69. *See also* collaborative interactions
    in First 20 Days, 35–36
    resistance to, 10, 47, 67–68
    in turn to your neighbor routines, 31, 34fig, 35–36
ping-pong and volleyball classroom scenarios, 57
Pink, Daniel, 47–48, 53, 56, 64
planned ignoring of negative behaviors, 46
plasticity of brain, 21, 43
positive behavior interventions and supports (PBIS), 5–6, 71–72
positive behavior support (PBS), xi
power, culture of, 10, 63–64
POW-TREE strategy, 29
Presley, N., 63
problem-solving
    multiple entry points in, 54–62
    routines in, 28, 29
Probst, R., 57
procrastination, 55
productive struggle, engagement in, 56, 58–59, 61, 62–63
professional learning community, instructional calendars in, 85, 91, 93
progress monitoring and reteaching in scaffolding executive function, 35, 37–39, 40
    feedback in, 38
    instructional practices checklist on, 5fig
    learning map on, 12fig
    roster checklist in, 37–38, 38fig, 87
    student self-assessments in, 38
prosocial behaviors, 6
    explicit instruction of, 63–65
Proust, Marcel, 7, 8
purpose, perceived feelings of
    in collaborative community, 63–65

definition of, 51
and motivation, 48, 49fig, 51–53, 56, 63–65
in multiple entry points, 56

questions
student preparation of, for classroom discussions, 74–75, 76–78
teacher preparation of advancing and assessing questions, 60–61
Questions Planning Template, 74
quick write routine, 103fig, 105fig

ramp-up periods, 86–87, 94
reflection
on classroom discussion in Socratic Seminar, 77–80
on First 20 Days routines, 31–34
in instructional calendar review, 86–87
in SCORE strategy, 69
in try, fail, try again cycle, 69–70
research-based practices, 4
resistance of students, 10
in First 20 Days, 39
in math instruction, 44–47, 51, 60
to peer interactions, 10, 47, 67–68
response inhibition, 22, 23
responsibility, gradual release of, 3, 8, 9, 10
in First 20 Days, 34
in Socratic Seminar, 75–76, 77–78
roster checklist in progress monitoring, 37–38, 38fig, 87
routines
automaticity in, 25, 43
chunking activities in, 26–27
cognitive load reduced in, 32, 61–62, 73–74
in communication and collaboration, 28, 29
coronavirus pandemic affecting, 8–9
critical, 5fig, 12fig, 28–30, 40
in First 20 Days. *See* First 20 Days routines

for grade-level content, 39
and habits, 21
importance of, 26–27
in learning, 28, 29
monitoring progress and reteaching of, 5fig, 37–39
in multistep tasks, 30
organizational, 28, 29, 88
in SCORE strategy, 64–69
in Socratic Seminar, 71, 73–74, 75–80
at start-of-class, 13–19, 28, 29
useful, 27–28
verbal rehearsal of, 28
Ryan, R., 53, 56, 64, 69

scaffolding, 1
of executive function, 13–41. *See also* executive function
of motivation, 11, 43–81. *See also* motivation
SCORE strategy, 29, 64–69, 76, 79–80
growth mindset in, 66–67
in instructional calendar, 102fig
skills in, 66fig
in small groups, 66–67
think time in, 67–69
scripts, 69–70
self-control, 9
response inhibition in, 22, 23
Self-Determination Theory: Basic Psychological Needs in Motivation, Development, and Wellness (Ryan & Deci), 53
self-efficacy, developing sense of, 24
multiple entry points in, 61, 62
self-talk of students, and internal motivation, 44
Sherin, M., 56, 59, 60, 61
short-term memory, 27
Simonsen, B., 72
sleep deprivation, 8–9
smartphone use, 8, 9
Smith, Fran, xi–xii
Smith, M., 56, 59, 60, 61

social skills
    and interpersonal behaviors, 6, 7–8, 9
    and prosocial behaviors, 6, 64
    SCORE strategy on, 64–69
Socratic Seminar, 71, 73–74, 76–80
    reflection sheet in, 79fig
spectator behavior
    in math instruction, 45, 57, 60
    in virtual instruction, 8
start-of-class routines, 13–19, 28, 29
Strategic Instruction Model (SIM), 30, 32
Student Learning Communities: A Springboard for Academic and Social Development (Fisher, Frey, & Almarode), 44
student ownership of learning, 4, 10
student–teacher relationships in First 20 Days, 31
success of students, barriers and obstacles to, 8–11
sustained attention, 22, 23

task difficulty
    in complex and multistep tasks. *See* complex and multistep tasks
    and engagement in productive struggle, 56, 58–59, 61
    in "Goldilocks" tasks, 53, 56
    and risk of failure, 59–61
task initiation, 22, 23
    autonomy in, 50
    hook for students in, 56, 58
    multiple entry points in, 11, 54–62, 80–81
    procrastination in, 55
    resistance to, 47, 51, 60
teachers
    assessing and advancing questions prepared by, 60–61
    circulation in classroom. *See* circulation of teachers in classroom
    expectations in beginning1of-class routines, 13–19
    as expert learners, 63
    in ping-pong and volleyball classroom scenarios, 57
    and student relationships in First 20 Days, 31
    try, reflect, try again cycle for, 47
Teach Like a Champion (Lemov), 29, 32
text annotation, 15, 17, 18, 29
    Annotation Poster on, 90
    instructional calendar on, 103fig, 104fig
    motivation in, 50
    Notice and Note strategy, 29
    in Socratic Seminar, 76–77, 78–79
    in THIEVES, 17, 18
THIEVES mnemonic, 17, 18fig
    in instructional calendar, 89fig, 102fig, 103fig
Think Draw or Write routine, 88–89
Think-Pair routine, 28, 29, 88, 89
    in instructional calendar, 103fig, 105fig
Think-Pair-Square and Share, 89, 103fig, 105fig
think time
    in preparation for classroom discussions, 74–75
    in SCORE strategy, 67–69
3 Big Questions routine in instructional calendar, 104fig, 105fig, 106fig
Tier 1 systems, xii, 97
time-management skills, 3
Total Participation Techniques (Himmele & Himmele), 29
try, fail, try again cycle
    growth mindset in, 4, 69–70
    mastery-oriented feedback in, 69–71
    motivation in, 44
    as necessary part of learning, 4
try, reflect, try again cycle for teachers, 47
turn to your neighbor (TTYN) routines, 29, 31, 34fig, 35–36
    low-risk, 35–36
    in math class scenario, 45
21st century learning goals, 50, 52

communication and collaboration in, 62–63, 74
limitations of extrinsic motivation in, 48
mastery-oriented feedback in, 72–73

Universal Design for Learning (UDL), xi–xiii, 1–5, 92fig
  on collaboration, 62–64
  on grade-level content, 39
  Guideline 6 in, 3, 5, 9, 83, 91
  Guideline 8 in, 3–4, 5, 9, 62–63, 83, 91
  instructional models based on, xiii, 5, 9
  learner variability in, 22–23, 91
  as lens, xii, 2–3
  on mastery-oriented feedback, 69, 74
  on multiple entry points, 56
  obstacles removed by intentional design in, 54
University of Kansas Center for Research on Learning's Strategic Instruction Model (KU-CRL SIM), 30

Van de Walle, J., 56
virtual instruction during coronavirus pandemic, 8–10
visual scaffolds, 30
volleyball and ping-pong classroom scenarios, 57

working memory
  capacity of, 20, 21, 25
  chunking tasks in, 11
  cognitive load in, 21, 32, 43
  daily challenges in, 20–21
  definition of, 20, 23
  individual differences in, 22–23
  instructional practices checklist on, 5fig
  learning map on, 12fig
  in multistep tasks, 19–21, 24–25, 26
  phone number digits in, 20
  in routines, 28, 32
  scaffolding of, 4, 12fig, 21, 24, 25–28, 40, 41
Would You Rather routine, 89, 103fig, 105fig

zone of proximal development, 9

More from CAST Professional Publishing

UDL Now! A Teacher's Guide to Applying Universal Design for Learning, Third Edition

By Katie Novak, with a foreword by George Couros

"Katie Novak's well-articulated know-how, about how to put UDL into practice, has helped many thousands of educators . . . She can describe what she does without evaporating the awe, the joy, or the sublimity of what great teaching is really like."

—DAVID H. ROSE, co-founder of CAST

ISBN 978-1-930583-82-5 (Print)
ISBN 978-1-930583-83-2 (ePub)
196 PAGES | © 2022

Transform Your Teaching with Universal Design for Learning: Six Steps to Jumpstart Your Practice

By Jennifer L. Pusateri

"Putting UDL into practice can be daunting for teachers who are just starting out. Jennifer L. Pusateri puts them at ease as she suggests step-by-step strategies to transform our teaching with this powerful framework."

—ANDRATESHA FRITZGERALD, founder of Building Blocks of Brilliance LLC

ISBN 978-1-930583-95-5 (Print)
ISBN 978-1-930583-94-8 (ePub)
224 PAGES | © 2022

Unlearning: Changing Your Beliefs and Your Classroom with UDL

By Allison Posey and Katie Novak

"[The authors] not only take on system reform but ask us to examine our embedded beliefs of what learning is. They encourage readers to be bold and assertive in examining their assumptions, by creating space for self-discovery and sharing insights from their own journeys."

—BRYAN DEAN, UDL Innovation Specialist

ISBN 978-1-930583-44-3 (Print)
ISBN 978-1-930583-47-4 (ePub)
128 PAGES | © 2020

For more information, visit **www.castpublishing.org** or wherever books are sold. For bulk orders, email **publishing@cast.org**.

More from CAST Professional Publishing

Antiracism and Universal Design for Learning: Building Expressways to Success

By Andratesha Fritzgerald, with a foreword by Samaria Rice

"Fritzgerald offers very practical suggestions for making inclusion, antiracism, and the acceptance of differences the first and most important step in lesson planning... This book gives me hope that, in education, we can begin to eliminate the violence of academic and social prejudice that kills the spirit of our babies and belittles the needs and experiences of people of color."

—SAMARIA RICE, founder and CEO of the Tamir Rice Foundation

ISBN 978-1-930583-70-2 (Print)
ISBN 978-1-930583-71-9 (ePub)
192 PAGES | © 2020

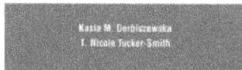

Supercharge Your Professional Learning: 40 Practical Strategies that Improve Adult Learning

By Kasia M. Derbiszewska and T. Nicole Tucker-Smith

"Drawing on their passion for staff development and deep knowledge of best practices, including UDL, the authors offer a power-packed guide to professional learning that is both rewarding and fun."

—JENNIFER LEVINE, Chief Academic Officer, CAST

ISBN 978-1-930583-74-0 (Print)
ISBN 978-1-930583-39-9 (ePub)
126 PAGES | © 2020

Elli: A Day in the Life of a Kid with ADHD

By Ari H.G. Yates

"My name is Elli, and this book is about me! I'm 9 years old and I have ADHD. In this book, I want to explain what it's like having ADHD, the bad and the good. Maybe another kid can read this book and realize that many others have ADHD, and even though it can be difficult, you can still accomplish a lot of cool things... Especially if you understand your ADHD better!"

—A message from Elli, who inspired the book

ISBN 978-1-930583-90-0 (Print)
ISBN 978-1-930583-91-7 (ePub)
40 PAGES | © 2021

For more information, visit **www.castpublishing.org** or wherever books are sold. For bulk orders, email **publishing@cast.org**.

MORE FROM CAST

CAST is a nonprofit education research and development organization that created the Universal Design for Learning framework and UDL Guidelines. Our mission is to transform education design and practice until learning has no limits.

CAST supports learners and educators at every level through a variety of offerings:

- Innovative professional development
- Accessibility and inclusive technology resources
- Research, design, and development of inclusive and effective solutions
- Credentials for Universal Design for Learning
- And much more

Visit *www.cast.org* to learn more.